Denomii

CH00863075

A fraction of what happened
in one mathematics classroom

Available from
www.denominator.co.uk

by Jonny Griffiths

website: **www.jonny-griffiths.net**
email: *hello@jonny-griffiths.net*
twitter: @maxhikorski

First edition

ISBN: 978-0-244-72679-9

For Yvonne

There are three rules to writing a good memoir.
Unfortunately nobody knows what they are.

After W. Somerset Maugham (1874–1965)

Mathematics education is much more complicated than you expect,
even if you expect it to be much more complicated than you expect.

Edward G. Begle (1914–78)

People often say, 'I teach them but they don't learn.'
Well, if you know that, stop teaching.
I don't mean resign from your job;
stop teaching in a way that doesn't reach people.

Caleb Gattegno (1911–88)

What follows is a mixture of what happened,
what I wish had happened,
and what I'm glad did not happen
in my classroom.

The students I taught were by and large on this trajectory;

Primary school (age 5-10);
Secondary school, ending with GCSE exams (age 11-15);
Sixth form college, ending with A Levels (age 16-18).
Many then went on to university, others found jobs.

O Levels were replaced a good while ago by GCSEs.

There are other pathways for UK students.

The UK education system is in a constant state of flux.

Demolition Time

'It's sad to see the old place go,' I say politely.

'I don't know.' Ruth, my ex-colleague, grins. 'To be honest, I'd love to be driving the first JCB that pulls this bloody dump to bits.'

I'm juggling a teacup, a plate and a scone as we chat. I look around the school hall that's hosting this bunfest; it looks even more beaten up than when I taught here. Through the window, the concrete slabs that provide the school with walls and paths are looking forlorn in the wind and rain. They seem to know their days are numbered.

I sigh. The school crest still sits proudly above the entrance to St Philip Howard Comprehensive in Tower Hamlets, and once upon a time, I'd walked eagerly beneath it to begin my teaching career. I left after a year and a half, and now a year after that there's been 'a reorganisation.' The school hasn't made the cut, and men in grey suits have reallocated the pupils elsewhere. Paula, my robust old Head, decided three months ago to bow out in celebratory fashion, throwing this goodbye party for all students and staff, past and present. Luckily not everyone wanted to come, which means there are still plenty of scones left. Attending for me now feels like returning to the scene of a mugging, but here I am, hoping for an overdue sense of closure.

I spot two young Vietnamese girls discussing something animatedly and pointing in my direction. I recognise them immediately as Kim and Qui, two delightful students I'd taught in my final months. Tower Hamlets had taken in a number of boat people, refugees from the appalling warring in South-East Asia, and these two girls had been randomly washed into my class. Their calm temperaments were in

4

noticeable contrast to those of my usual clientele. Kim once spoke for me as I came across a delicious poster created in my lesson, saying, 'Sir, that must be like roses for a maths teacher.' I had much the same feeling when marking the pair's immaculate exercise books.

Qui now breaks away from her partner, summons up courage and walks in my direction. Her thirteen-year-old face gazes up questioningly, her vast eyes seeking out mine.

'Did you used to be Mr Griffiths?' she asks.

As I write this paragraph now, it is twenty-five years on from Qui's question. The time is four o'clock on the last day of the Summer Term, 2015, and I've taught my final lesson at the sixth form college where I've worked for many years. With choking emotion I've said goodbye to my colleagues and limped home. I'm now juggling not tea-time accoutrements, but waves of relief, anxiety and mild depression. Yes, I used to be Mr Griffiths.

It's not too early to be asking some big questions. What were the best bits? The worst? Was I actually any good? Given my time again, would I choose to be a teacher? Will any of my students remember me? For what reasons? More mundanely, how many lessons in total did I actually teach? And what's my life expectancy now that I've finally stepped off the educational roller-coaster?

The days and then weeks of my retirement pass. Some questions refuse to go away. One in particular pushes itself to the front of the queue and repeats itself until I have to stop and listen. 'What actually happened there? Could you reflect on that, Jonny, for a minute or two?'

I loved the job, at least the job I ended up with. I loved engaging with students, who supplied a constant stream of entertainment as we slalomed together through the syllabus. I loved my subject; the mystical beauty of mathematics grew daily more apparent to me as I taught. And I love the question, 'How do you best bring young people and maths together?' It's one of the profoundest there is. Maths and me, me and my students, my students and mathematics, three relationships that on a good day danced together in my classroom.

But on a bad day, teaching can go wrong. Even the most successful teacher (maybe especially the most successful teacher) has a life of huge stresses, aching sadnesses and perceived failures. Caroline was an extraordinary art teacher, making the end of year student exhibition look more like the contents of a London art gallery than an obligatory show in a college theatre. But yet she could be unpopular with her students.

'They say I make too many demands,' she told me once, with a heavy sigh. I've seen top teachers shaking with worry as they arrive on Results Day (it's often said that this date in the calendar is harder for the teacher than the student, but clichés are usually true). If the joys of teaching beat those of any other profession, then the lows can be more crippling than those elsewhere too.

So this is a book about mathematics, and one about teaching young adults, and also one about the curious outcomes that result when you try to mix the two. These themes may not immediately be your bag, but I invite you to keep an open mind. I'm not writing for maths specialists or for teaching professionals, but for those curious about what maths teaching actually felt like to one ordinary joe, myself.

.

My life at St Philip Howard in Poplar is one tale in this book, a narrative from a school where I lasted 18 months. I should say that back at the end of the 1980s, Tower Hamlets education was in the doldrums. The transformation in achievement across London schools in the early twenty-first century was one of the most admirable miracles ever seen in the public sector. From being the worst-performing in the UK, London schools became the best. The reasons are many and complex, but you should know that the school I taught in back then and the schools that were available in Tower Hamlets in the 2010s are different in the extreme.

The chronicles of my first steps as a teacher in East London are interwoven with stories from the generally steadier twenty-three years I had teaching sixth formers at Paston College in Norfolk. The Tower Hamlets pieces are always flagged up as such in the first line or two and are in the past tense, while the Norfolk pieces are all in the present tense. I also throw in the occasional more general piece inspired by mathematics itself, in the hope that you'll be tempted to listen to the queen of the sciences; she'll reward your attention, I promise. If you feel your maths might not be up to it, then I hope to surprise you.

So this is my story; every teacher has one. I can't promise you a happy ending; it most certainly has a painful beginning. But then again, I can't change a thing, and what's more (long pause) I wouldn't want to.

I Have a Request

It's Tuesday morning at Paston College, and I'm addressing my GCSE resit class, twenty students who managed a D or lower first time around, and who are now seeking that elusive grade C (officially seen as a pass) once again.

'Hello, folks, and I have some good news: I've been asked to write some pieces for a maths teaching journal.'

'A maths – teaching – journal?' says Toby, incredulous. 'Can such a thing exist?'

'They'll publish anything nowadays,' says Kate cheerily.

This is not going quite as planned.

'The point is, I'd like to be able to mention anything that happens in this classroom. Is that okay with you all? I will, of course, change your names.'

'Hey, can I be Biggles?' asks Roger enthusiastically.

'Penelope Pitstop for me, please,' says Louise.

I decide to take this as a 'Yes,' and move on.

'We've also been asked to appear in a reality TV show called GCSE Maths Bootcamp, what do you think?' I add lightly, which gets the confused silence I'm hoping for. 'So how about some maths?'

There are the usual problems with pens. 'Can I borrow a pen, please?' says Amy plaintively.

I sigh, and ask if anyone has a pen they can lend her.

'Sure,' says Robert warmly, and a pen is passed across.

It is exam preparation time, my students are tackling past papers, and I do a hopeful calculation to psyche myself up.

'I'm allowing ten 90–minute lessons for past papers,' I say to myself, 'and if I intervene once a minute, with every intervention producing one extra mark for that student, then for a class of twenty, over the ten lessons that's 45 marks improvement each, and that's not including the incredible idea that some students might learn something without talking to me! Maybe they WILL all pass!'

My students' mistakes turn out to be more revealing than their correct answers. Vicky has tackled this question: 'Write $\frac{1}{16}$ as a decimal.' I pause – I think this is hard, on the paper where calculators are outlawed. Maybe Vicky is meant to say this;

$$\frac{1}{2} \text{ is } 0.5000$$

$$\frac{1}{4} \text{ is } 0.2500$$

$$\frac{1}{8} \text{ is } 0.1250$$

$$\frac{1}{16} \text{ is } 0.0625.$$

She has in fact written as her answer $\frac{1}{16} = \mathbf{0.16.}$ It seems to me that there are good things about her decimal. It is better than 1.6, which is bigger than 1. But surely $\frac{1}{16}$ is less than a tenth? Maybe 0.016 would have been better still?

I have a quick think. Vicky has come up with this rule – to find the decimal for one over a number, you do nought point the number. This makes the maths teacher bit of me curious. Whether her rule is right or wrong, Vicky deserves credit for coming up with a conjecture and not simply guessing at random. So is her rule always true, sometimes true, or never true?

Time for a plenary. The class quickly get the hang of what Vicky is suggesting. She blushes with the attention. We experiment a little.

'Hey, $\frac{1}{10}$ is 0.10: so Vicky's rule does work!' says Lawrence.

'Nice, Lawrence; can we come up with a number less than 10 that works? What about $\frac{1}{2}$?' I ask.

'A half is 0.5, so that doesn't work; Vicky's rule says $\frac{1}{2}$ is 0.2, but that's too small.'

'Does it work for $\frac{1}{5}$?'

'The fraction $\frac{1}{5}$ equals 0.2, not 0.5, which is too big. So if 0.2 is too small and 0.5 is too big…' Rosemary's brow furrowed with effort. 'In that case, there must be a number somewhere between $\frac{1}{5}$ and $\frac{1}{2}$ that DOES work,' she concludes.

'Brilliant insight, Rosemary, thank you!' I say. The problem is turning into a nice trial and improvement one.

'We've got $\frac{1}{3.2} = 0.3125$,' offers Nicky, forgetting now the fact that calculators are not allowed. 'And $\frac{1}{3.125} = 0.32$.'

'Can someone give me a number between 3.2 and 3.125? Jessica?'

This is something of an effort, but she succeeds. '3.175?'

'And $\frac{1}{3.175} = 0.31496...$ do you notice these are closer?'

And so on, as far as we wish to go.

'How about some algebra on this?' I ask, to the inevitable groans, but we stick with it.

'We kind of need $\frac{1}{x}$ = 0.x,' I say. 'So that gives 1 = 0.x², if we multiply

by x.' Rigour has ceased to play any part here; I'm making up notation and simplifying wildly.

'And if we multiply by 10, we get x^2 = 10,' says Damien smartly. Hardly in the textbook, but he's right.

'So what's x?' I ask.

'We square root; that gives x = $\sqrt{10}$,' offers Lisa. 'Which is 3.16227...'

Everyone tries $\frac{1}{3.16227...}$ to find it equal to 0.316227... Simple stuff, but this final calculation has taken on the aspect of a magic trick.

'So was the algebra useful or not?' I ask, trying not to sound too smug. There are a couple of grudging murmurs along with some conciliatory mumbles.

Back to working on other questions, I see that Robert has apparently done nothing all lesson.

'Why haven't you written anything?' I ask, looking at his blank page.

'I gave my pen to Amy,' he says cheerfully.

I break my New Year's resolution not to call any student a plonker in 2014.

'A generous plonker, though, Robert...'

12

Mr Lanchester

Back in 1987, as I prepared to learn my trade in St Philip Howard School, it was hard not to wonder who'd been in my classroom before me, and why they'd left. I found out one day before I started; my predecessor was someone called Mr Lanchester, whose chaotic teaching style had impressed no-one. Margaret, my new Head of Department, comprehensively spilled the beans down the pub at lunchtime.

'He sent Jamie down to see me for throwing a book at him,' she said scornfully, as the Maths department sat around her, gripping pints. 'Now Jamie's a good kid. He said to me, "I just want to do some work, Miss, but I can't with all the others arsing about." What could I say?'

Apparently Mr Lanchester had spent most of his lessons up at the board with glazed eyes whispering to himself, while wild students reconstructed his classroom around him. It was rumoured that his sinister mantra was, 'You got my wife, you little bastards, but you won't get me.' Margaret kindly drew a veil over where Mr Lanchester was now.

My new colleagues roared with laughter, but my chortling was uneasy. As we drank up to get back to business, I gulped inwardly. Would I fare any better?

Writing Upside Down

It's a sunny day as I stroll across the courtyard to my lesson humming the song 'Skylark'. As I walk I'm idly reviewing my mental list entitled, 'What should have been in my teacher training that wasn't.' A practical algorithm, for example, for sorting a pile of a hundred reports into alphabetical order as swiftly as possible would have been more than handy. But at the top of my list always comes, 'How to write upside down'.

The situation is common. A teacher faces two students across a table, and needs to write down something mathematical. (Ideally the teacher would be alongside the two students, but the logistics of the seating may make that impossible.) Struggling to keep a million balls in the air at once, an inexperienced teacher writes as they normally would. They may not realise how hard it'll be for the students to understand, as they try to read the inverted text; these learners didn't take this on board the first time round the right way up. The teacher may be hoping that they will just catch on, but one day it dawns: the thing to do is to write upside down.

Students are always delighted when a teacher tries to do this. Comments, accompanied by peals of laughter, might be these:

'Is that supposed to be a 5?'

'Can't you go any faster?'

'Oh, look at that Z! Bless!'

Students love to see a teacher handicap themselves, perhaps because so often in the maths classroom they feel handicapped themselves. There's a sense of things being evened up, of a playing field being levelled. The students' job is to understand the maths, while the teacher's job is to write upside down correctly. If the teacher makes a mistake, it makes it harder for the student, and vice versa. There's a helpful sense of being all in the same boat.

So what if we try to write the capital letters upside down? Some are easy (X, H, O), some are fairly easy (A, Y, T), while some are a little harder (G, B and Q). Some are deceptive; it's tempting to write an N as an Ͷ. But when we practice N, S and Z, we discover these letters read the same whether they face you or your student. I like to think of these as mathematical truths that are unchanging however they are viewed. Maybe it's possible to try too hard to put yourself into your students' shoes. It is possible that in the process you may twist a truth into an untruth.

This question comes back to me from time to time; what will students remember about me when they look back? Kevin said appreciatively once, 'That Mr Lanchester, he had really yellow spit.' But I recall Natalie saying about Mrs Holmes, 'She could write upside down really fast.' With practice, one can indeed get remarkably quick at reflected writing.

This topic sometimes makes me regretful. When I write on the board, does the maths subtly face me? Could I write instead so that the maths faces my students, even if that makes it look strange from my point of view?

15

As turn the handle to my classroom door, I can see in my mind's eye that next to that list of 'Teacher Training Gaps' is a list of 'Metaphors for Teaching.' These vary in usefulness: the Teacher as Priest, initiating their Congregation into a body of Secret Knowledge, or the Teacher as Overflowing Jug, with the class cast as Empty Vessels, or the Teacher as Gardener, surrounded by their Heliotropic Young Plants. But as I scan down that list, I always, whatever the weather, seem to have the same favourite; Teaching as Writing Upside Down.

Craze

Every so often, a craze consumes an educational establishment, whether it's for a computer game, or friendship bracelets, or pink phone covers, or any of a million and one things. I watched such a phenomenon blow into my classroom on a Monday, dance around for a few days, and then disappear off again by the Friday without so much as a goodbye.

On Monday, white plastic Show Me Boards in see-through polythene wallets (modern-day slates, each with a pen and a sponge eraser) hang unremarkably from elastic bands on one of my walls.

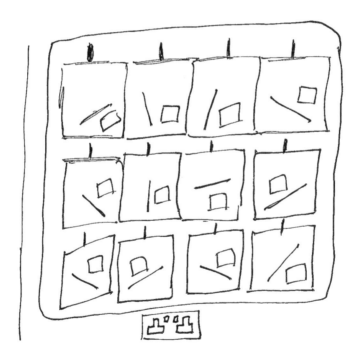

On Tuesday, someone makes a breakthrough.

With the help of the elastic band, a wallet can become, the discovery
goes, a surreal pendulum, one that rocks regularly in any light breeze.
The equilibrium is stable.

The craze kicks in. Wednesday sees lots of laughter as students catch
on. Thursday concludes like this…

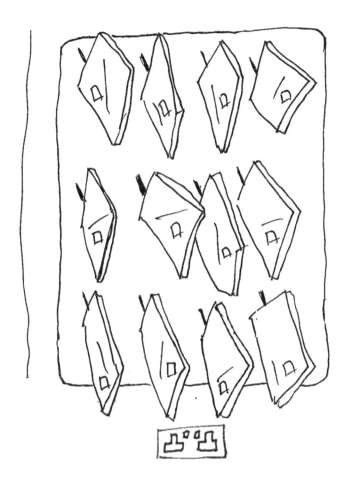

By Friday, this particular craze has, it seems, burned itself out.

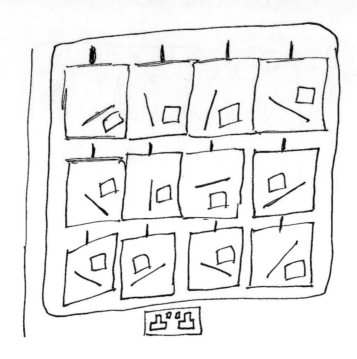

Slate-mania disappears as quickly as it arrives, and the boards quietly return to Monday's arrangement.

Hmm. How could I turn my subject into a craze? Permanently?

Then and Now

I joined my Norfolk sixth form college in 1992, and I said goodbye in 2015. As Jonny Leaving, I look back to the teacher I was, Jonny Arriving, and have an imaginary conversation...

'So, Jonny Leaving, what can you tell me about maths teaching in 2015? It's hard to imagine from back here. What's the big change?'

'That question, Jonny Arriving, is stunningly easy to answer. It's the advent of the computer.'

'We've got computers. Some Nimbus machines that we run Logo on.'

'Ah, but we now have computers in every room, all connected by a network. We still have the wonders of Logo, but lots of other programs too, for graphing, for spreadsheets, for games...'

'So can people communicate with each other using your network?'

'We have something called "email". Anyone can send a message to anyone else over the network, instantly.'

'That must save a lot of time!'

'Er... sometimes, Jonny Arriving, it does, but sometimes, strangely, it doesn't.'

'So what else have computers made possible?'

'My whiteboard has become computerised, or as we say, interactive. You can project all sorts of things onto your screen, anything that your computer screen can show. I can write with my electronic pen, I can refer back to earlier slides, and I can send out the paperless lesson notes to students afterwards. No more cleaning the board, and forget that overhead projector.'

'Welcome indeed. What happens if the computer goes wrong?'

'Er… that does, indeed, tend to be a bit of a disaster.'

'Anything else, Jonny Leaving, that I need to know?'

'Let me show you, Jonny Arriving, the internet! These are what we call websites, offering resources, videos, slide shows, an endless world of possibilities!'

'It's amazing that anyone still bothers to talk to anyone else in 2015. But surely these websites must be expensive to sign up for?'

'Most, including some of the best, are completely free.'

'It is hard to believe that mankind can be that generous.'

'It's true! No longer do your students need to lug around heavy textbooks. Here's a free maths site, for example, called Wolfram Alpha – just put in your question, and back comes the answer.'

'Will it integrate for you? I'll bet it can't do the integral of $e^{\sqrt{x}}$.'

'Back it comes, Jonny Arriving, with $2e^{\sqrt{x}}(\sqrt{x}-1)+c.$ Pretty damn quick.'

'So what must this mean for exams? Surely you're free with the help of these computers to ask some wonderfully imaginative questions! Liberated from the drudgery of doing all that calculation by hand, all that stuff that machines are so much better at than we are, students must be tackling questions about modelling, investigating, conjecturing; please, Jonny Leaving, show me the exam papers of the future! I want to be inspired!'

'Er... well, Jonny Arriving, I should say computers, proper computers, are not allowed in most exams. As for exam papers, you could have a look at this...'

'But... oh no! Isn't this the same as what WE do?'

Lesson One

The day had come, I could put it off no longer. I'd read all the books, I'd rung round for advice, I'd sorted through my wardrobe. This first lesson had been planned to extinction. I stood watchfully by my Tower Hamlets desk as the vanguard of the class came through the door.

'What the hell?'

The first trio were gazing open-mouthed at the board.

'It's a seating plan!' they squawked.

St Philip Howard clearly did not go in for such things, but hey, that made this a novelty. The twenty-five students gradually deciphered where they were meant to be, and while grumbling, manoeuvred themselves into position.

'These desks are weird!' said a girl caked in make-up, who already looked bored. I'd spent a week planning the optimum arrangement; it looked like the Hampton Court maze. Was that make-up allowed? I made a mental note to check later.

'Hello everybody, my name's Mr Griffiths, and I'm your new maths teacher!' I said brightly. 'And we'll start with a problem that I'm going to put on the board.'

I turned to rub off the seating plan, and I heard a voice clearly whisper, 'How long's he going to last?'

I turned quickly, and saw the 'miscreant', a small lad with alert eyes and a quizzical smile. I tried to correlate his position with my seating plan, and failed; my memory baulked under the pressure. I'd thought about discipline, of course, but at this stage, I had but a single tactic. I'd been blessed since youth with an astonishingly loud finger-click, and I directed one of these towards this obviously subversive element now.

Click! 'What's your name?' I said. There was a definite sense of confrontation in my voice.

After a stunned silence, the entire group burst into unrestrained laughter.

'Ha, ha, ha!' They clicked away themselves, and their twenty-four clicks proved to be louder than mine alone.

'What's your name?' they roared in imitation. The young lad I'd 'tackled', who turned out to be called Stephen, gazed at me in pity.

'What a jerk!' he said in amazement.

'You need to know that I am really determined!' I yelled. Mr Lanchester would have been proud of me.

The rest of the day went, let's say, badly. At its close, Margaret came into my room looking rueful, and kicked the desks into a more sensible shape. She talked through the systems that the Maths department had in place, and advised me to let those take the strain. I went home to regroup, only to wake at three in the morning with a mouth like sandpaper.

Little Bo Peep

How do you feel about infinity? If a mathematician were asked to describe her relationship with infinity, she might say, 'It's complicated.' Some adventurous heroes have brought insight into its study where there was none before, but others have set themselves infinity-inspired problems that seem to have done their health more harm than good.

It's generally agreed amongst mathematicians now that there are different kinds of infinity. The simplest kind is called 'countable'; can you put your infinity of objects into a list (an infinite one)? Clearly the positive whole numbers are countable, and the positive even numbers are too;

2, 4, 6, 8,...

What about ALL of the whole numbers, including the negative ones? We can put those into a comprehensive list with an obvious pattern too.

0, 1, -1, 2, -2, 3, -3, ...

Maybe we can put EVERY infinity of objects into a list that includes all the objects? It turns out that we can't; the infinity of numbers between 0 and 1, for example, that's all decimals between 0 and 1, cannot be put into a list; we say they are 'uncountable'. This is a bigger infinity than the infinity of whole numbers, as the German mathematician Cantor showed in 1891.

A question might occur to us; what about the fractions? The idea that there might be more fractions than whole numbers is appealing; we can always find lots of fractions between any two whole numbers, but we can't always find a whole number between any two fractions. So here's the key question; can we put all of the fractions into a list? The following story investigates this problem…

Little Bo Peep's business was booming. Sheep were in demand, and when it came to shepherdesses, there were none finer. She had, in fact, now been successful enough to collect an infinite number of sheep in her flock. Which in turn gave her a headache; how to count them?

*She'd tried putting **1, 2, 3, 4…** onto the side of each sheep in turn, and after a long while, during which she had become infinitely quick at painting a number onto the flank of a sheep, she'd managed to number them all, unlikely as that may sound. This did not, however, completely answer her problem.*

*'Bo Peep,' said a local farmer, sounding exasperated. 'We paint **1, 2, 3, 4…** onto the sides of OUR sheep. How can we tell yours and ours apart?'*

Bo Peep's forehead creased as she grappled with this conundrum. Then it came to her in a flash; 'I'll paint fractions onto the sides of my sheep!'

The next day, she set to work. 'Every sheep must have a fraction, and every fraction must correspond to a sheep', she thought. 'I'll count $\frac{1}{1}, \frac{2}{2}, \frac{3}{3}$ … as the same fraction; equivalent fractions like these must only occur once, in their simplest form!' she cried. 'In addition, I must be able to put my sheep in some kind of order.'

But how could she do this? Immediately she was struck with a dilemma; what would happen if she tried to arrange her sheep in order of size?

'Suppose I have all my sheep lined up in order of size, and suppose sheep $\frac{a}{b}$ and $\frac{c}{d}$ are next to each other. Now between any two sheep $\frac{a}{b}$ and $\frac{c}{d}$ comes the sheep $\frac{a+c}{b+d}$,' she realised, despairingly. 'For example, between $\frac{5}{7}$ and $\frac{3}{4}$ is $\frac{8}{11}$. So they won't be next door to each other, and I have a contradiction; I can never line all my sheep up in order of size.'

She went for a hike to clear her head. As she looked down onto her flock from the top of a nearby fell, it came to her suddenly.

'I'll use a different kind of order! A fraction can give birth to two others, like this!' she cried.

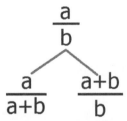

'Now if I start with $\frac{1}{1}$, I get this tree of fractions, branching out to infinity.'

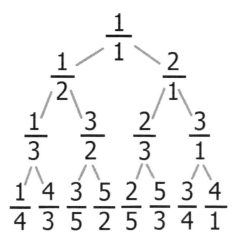

'I think I can see that every fraction will occur just once, in its simplest form, although the proof of this is indeniably tricky!' she conceded. 'Now if I put the rows together in a long line, I've got my sheep in an order that works!'

That afternoon, she set to with a paint brush. Sadly, she found that there were side–effects to counting her flock. Two hours later, a passing shepherd found her, fast asleep...

Michael

It's four o'clock, the end of our performing day, and when the paperwork starts. My weary Paston colleagues and I are slowly unwinding in the Maths Office, as David puts on the kettle. He's our Head of Department, and we're blessed indeed. He'd walk over nails for any of us, and for any of his students too. He's the embodiment of fatherliness, in the most proper of ways.

I'm sipping my tea when there's a knock on the door. David takes a look.

'Yes, Michael?' he says, flashing me a warning glance.

'Could I have a quick word with Jonny, please?' says a bright, nervous voice. I don't sigh, but inwardly I think, 'Is that my quick or yours, Michael?' It's the eighth time Michael has knocked on the door asking for me in three weeks.

I guess most of the aggravation in a teacher's life (not counting hassle from management and the government) arises from students who lack motivation. But there is another student who can be just as draining. I am thinking of the Over–Motivated Student, the Driven, Obsessed Student, the one who is likely to worry themselves into a premature grave in advance of the very exams they are worrying about. Michael's a case in point. Heading towards a maths degree at a prestigious university, he scored a high grade A on both his Maths AS and his Further Maths AS last year. When the results for the first module of the A2 year arrived, he'd once more scored an A.

'Pleased with your C3 score, Michael?' I'd asked.

'No,' he said, his face creased with anxiety. 'I only <u>just</u> got an A.'

Now Michael is staying behind after college once more to seek my reassurance.

'It's just that I keep making silly mistakes,' he pleads. 'A minus sign missing here, and a wrong factorisation there; I don't want to fail to get an A just through silly mistakes.'

'But Michael, we all make silly mistakes,' I said. 'You watch me making mistakes all the time in class. Some are just careless, but some are actually helpful, in a strange way. Why are you so afraid of making mistakes?'

'It's just that I know I can get an A, I've set my heart on it.'

Normally with an anxious student I'll sit down together, go through the mark-book, and see what the picture really is. If their anxiety is justified, we form a plan, and if it's not, their marks should speak. In both cases they leave relieved, or at least more balanced. I've tried this common-sense approach with Michael, and it's failed. I now have a problem; I teach a hundred students a week, and I need to share my emotional resources between them more or less equally. Michael is currently hogging more than his fair share.

'I've started to cover the wall of my room with yellow post–its,' he says earnestly.

I have a sudden vision of Michael's bedroom looking like an advert for Kraft cheese slices. I can stand no more.

31

'Apart from you, Michael, who cares what you get in your A level?' I ask firmly.

His bambi eyes look at me in a bewildered way, as if he's just seen me kick a puppy.

'I mean, I care, of course,' I add swiftly, 'But what's better, to go to Cambridge with three As and hate it, or to go to Bangor with three Cs and love it?'

Michael was still too stunned to reply.

'Look, Michael,' I said gently. 'The world is your oyster. It needs more good mathematicians than it has. University maths departments will be fighting over you. After that, employers will be. You are gold dust. Just enjoy being seventeen.'

The next day, the Further Maths A2 group and I are tackling a piece of maths together.

'Michael, what did you get for the final answer?' I ask.

'Two,' he says.

'Shouldn't that be plus or minus two?' says Charlotte.

She's right. I look at Michael.

'Come on, you can do it,' I think.

I see him jump in a frightened way, but then a smile crosses his face.

'Just give me the revolver,' he says calmly. 'I've brought disgrace on myself and my family. I know what I have to do…'

After my dose of shock therapy, Michael put his worry to one side, got his sense of humour back, and stopped using me as an inappropriate crutch. He was awarded top grades at A Level, and went on to read maths at one of the best universities. Job done.

Can I Help?

It was Day Two in my St Philip Howard classroom. Someone had his hand up.

'Hello, so you are?' I asked politely. I'd learnt something from yesterday. I moved towards his table.

'I'm Alex.' A face that was older than its years looked me up and down. I was the latest in a string of teachers for this group; would I be any good? He sniffed and decided to give me a chance.

'What's the problem?' I asked.

'I don't know how to make this bigger,' he said.

The task required enlarging a shape. To do this, you had to pick a centre of enlargement, and draw lines from here through the corners of the shape to create a kind of skeleton for the enlarged figure. I was battling with a sense of vertigo. The classroom felt strange, there were odd noises coming from all corners of it, and on top of this, I couldn't make head or tail of the question. My own school mathematics education had been entirely traditional fare, based around that far-sighted Greek Euclid, who'd sadly not foreseen my current predicament. What was required here was transformation geometry, a gap in my knowledge that my degree had done nothing to rectify.

'Er…' I floundered.

'Maybe if I did this?' offered Alex.

'Yes, good idea,' I muttered hopefully. 'And I think if you draw this line...'

'No, look, it's this one,' said Alex. 'It's all right, I've got it now.'

'Good. Just - give a shout, Alex, if you've got any more problems,' I said weakly.

'Yeah, whatever,' he said.

I moved on to my next pupil, and as I turned, I heard Alex say wearily to his neighbour, 'That's all we need; a thick teacher.'

As some kind of penance that evening, I stayed late in my corridor with a roll of red tape creating an enlargement of my classroom door.

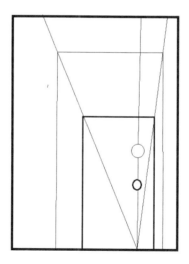

35

Brighter Than Me

Twenty-five years on, and I'm surveying my GCSE resit class as they work busily on exactly the same mathematics that Alex asked me to help him with back then. The scrape of rulers on squared paper is all I can hear. The task is to enlarge a quadrilateral, and my students are absorbed. I've got to grips with transformation geometry since Alex wrote me off (it still rankles), and it seems I've explained myself successfully enough today. *If I tried to support the young tyke again, I hope I'd actually do so,* I think. But Alex makes me ask; suppose the student IS brighter than the teacher? Is this a disaster, or an opportunity?

I reflect on what's needed to get into my current college. Paston has a generous admissions policy; no one could call the place elitist. But we attract many high-fliers, and a steady handful of students try for Oxbridge in a standard year. Our A Level maths groups are a mixed bunch, yet I always find myself teaching two or three students who I consider to be seriously bright, who could, should they choose that path, become more effective mathematicians than I am.

Down the years, I've identified two types of brighter–than–the–teacher students. Nigel, for example (and it's usually a boy), will take in my equation on the board, and say, looking round triumphantly at his colleagues, 'Don't you mean one over x CUBED, Jonny?' He doesn't mean to be irritating, but the smugness in his voice leaves me muttering under my breath, 'Smart-arses in that corner, please, Nigel…'

But Nora, the second kind of bright student, instead says kindly, 'Jonny, I like your equation,' (pause for me to preen) 'but I'm just wondering, could it be improved?' She smiles quizzically, which cues laughter that even I can join in with.

Sometimes you get a third kind of response; 'You've made a mistake, Jonny, you're our teacher, and you're not supposed to do that.' An ugly spirit of accusation pervades the air. The only way out of this, I've found, is a bit of choice Anglo-Saxon. 'Oh, bollocks!' is enough to puncture the atmosphere and restore normality. In fact, I honestly don't know how those who say you should never swear in a sixth form classroom actually manage the job.

I look around my room again. This is one of those blessed moments where everyone is working without any help from me. Yes, Nora, the brighter–than–me but humble student, is a joy to teach, while Nigel, the brighter–than–me but competitive student, is harder work.

Mind you, I reflect, teachers can be competitive too. At Mrs G's school, management one Christmas came up with the misguided idea of a prize for the best-decorated classroom. Several teachers took the challenge seriously, but with a week to go there were two clear front-runners, Collette and Anna, whose classrooms daily groaned with new supplies of baubles and tinsel. With 48 hours to go, Collette thought she'd clinched it as she manoeuvred a life-size reindeer into place, only for Anna to arrive ten minutes before the judging with a snow-machine. Don't ask what kind of lessons these teachers were delivering in the week leading up to this.

My Guardian Angel whispers in my ear now as I gaze briefly out of my classroom window at the College gardener mowing the lawns below.

'Jonny, don't try,' she says, 'to outdo those of your students who would overtake you. Put your insecurities about your own brightness to one side, and rejoice in your students' brighter–than–you–ness.'

At last a hand goes up. It's Lee's, and I head in his direction. *Indeed, if my students aren't being bright, then whose fault is that?* I think, as I negotiate desks. *Maybe I'm teaching the lesson in a way that doesn't allow them to be bright. And should I be aiming for brightness or cleverness? I want to create clever mathematicians, ones who are hopefully cleverer than me, but also ones who are bright enough to have their feet on the ground.*

I reach Lee's table, we sort his problem, and I look around my room again.

For there are lots of people in the world, I reflect, *who are certainly clever without, unfortunately, being particularly bright. In fact, isn't this one of the more pressing problems the world has to face?*

Pie

If I've discovered one thing in teaching, it's this: it's useful to have a past. Students love to whisper in hushed tones about what their teachers did before (as they see it) giving up on real life and falling back on the classroom. You may remember Alan Pascoe, who won the 400 metre hurdles gold in the 1974 Commonwealth Games. He found work in my school when I was eleven, and perhaps because sport could not quite fill his days, he became my geography teacher. He would monogram the front of my book when he issued me with a text at the start of each year, and I treasured those initials. He also taught us rugby, and on one occasion sprinted across half the pitch so fast that the posts seemed to sway in the breeze. He left to become a multi-millionaire, but that's another story.

So what was my dark pre–teaching secret? There were many, I confess, but one was this: in the early nineties, I played a character called Stringfellow on a childrens' television programme (the gag was that Stringfellow would attempt to play any stringed instrument that he could lay his hands on).

There was a time when no self-respecting five-year-old would miss *Playdays* for the world. This meant that each year in my classes, a student would put up his hand up at about October–time. Expecting a question on algebra, I'd say, 'Yes?' only to hear, 'Were you really on *Playdays*, Jonny?'

Mrs G even gets the same from wide–eyed eleven–year–olds at her High School a full fifteen miles away.

'Do you know Stringfellow?'

She now replies, 'I don't only know him, I get to sleep with him.'

Student demands for a screening of the videos were commonplace; I met them with, 'When we get to Christmas.' It once transpired come Yuletide that they had *Playdays* mixed up with *The Magic Roundabout*, and thought I was the voice of the hairy dog.

My past often led to requests for a song, and why not? A teacher can turn such a plea to their advantage, for certainly, a lyric can be a handy hook on which to hang a piece of mathematics. Hence *Pie*, the song below, that aims to cement the idea of a radian into a young mathematician's mind.

In case you've never met a radian, it's a unit with which to measure angle, one that's necessary to make sense of more advanced mathematics. Early on in our mathematics careers, the unit we use for angle is the degree (of which there are 360 in a whole turn), and that idea never fully fades out of the mathematician's mind, but calculus (that's finding the gradient of a curve, or the area under a curve) does require sterner stuff over angles.

So what's a radian? Imagine you are at the centre O of a circle, radius r. You walk out a distance r to the edge of the circle on a straight line, reaching A. Then you turn left and walk around the circle, also a distance r, reaching B. The angle AOB is now exactly one radian (this turns out to be about 57.3°).

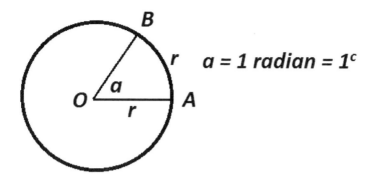

$a = 1 \text{ radian} = 1^c$

So here we go, pardners! The genre is Country and Western, there's a chorus that folk can sing along to, and if I say so myself, the applause is usually deafening.

Joe stood up at the Sunday lunch, in the bosom of his loving family,
With a slice in his hand, for the apple pie,
To serve his wife, and his daughter, and his fine sons three.
He said, 'How much?' to each in turn,
And they each said 'Sixty degrees!'
'Now six times sixty makes an empty plate,' thought Joe,
'That's my kind of maths, yes please!'
But then he came to his youngest son, who loved to get his father mad.
When Joe said 'How much?' this is what he heard:
'I'd like a radian, Dad!'

What's the point in a radian? If you know, please won't you tell?
Who needs a new–fangled unit?
When degrees have served us so well?
You say it'll make things easier, and I suppose that pigs might fly.
So how do I get an empty plate,
When I'm cutting up my Sunday lunch pie?

41

His son piped up, 'Let me tell you, radians are cool, and here's why.
Just look what they do to your formulae,
Remembering them's as easy as pie.
I like the crust, and to find its length, the radius times the angle will do,
And the area's easy to find as well, it's theta r squared over two.
So come on Dad, get with it, degrees are a little passé;
Okay, so the plate won't be empty,
But that's some more for another day.

Let's all use a radian, yes, a radian, why not risk it?
Nothing against the good old degree, but the radian takes the biscuit,
Those formulae look just nice and neat,
make 'em yours! You'll be in clover.
And the best thing about a radian,
** is that it leaves a bit of pie left over!**

This all leads to the nice question;

If all six members of the family choose a radian,
how much pie (in degrees) is left over?

(Left as an exercise for the reader.)

*Warning; there may be a video of **The Radian Song** somewhere on Youtube…*

Setting out together

Looking around furtively at my Tower Hamlets colleagues at our first staff meeting, I could count a number who were my kind of age. Indeed, it didn't take long to work out that five of us were starting our probationary year together. The others were all fresh off teaching courses; bubbly Carol in English, lanky Richard in Maths alongside me, witty Alice in Domestic Science, and even lankier Simon in Des and Tech.

Two weeks in, and it was safe to say none of us was finding things easy. We had our lessons to prepare from scratch, with no bank of previously-employed resources to call upon, and plenty of marking was piling up. This might have been manageable in the time available, but you had to factor in the stress. There was something about the noise created by a barely-controlled class that was astonishingly destructive. My first job on getting home was to lie flat on the floor for an hour to allow waves of psychological damage to stream off me like so much malignant radiation.

The eighteen months I spent in Tower Hamlets saw stress levels within me that I could only match with accounts of the Somme. Shell-shock was a daily reality. In the band I'd read lots, but in my first term of teaching I managed just one book, an account of Scott's journey towards death in the Antarctic. It fitted; I reached half-term just as they reached a supply dump. I started out in Tower Hamlets with no girlfriend, and I saw no point in trying to find one; how could I inflict this on her?

Was all of this good for us in any sense? Some observers thought it might be a kind of spiritual purification. My friend Jenny said to me one day, 'You know you're doing the right thing, don't you?' I said in reply,

'I'm just not sure that I'm psychologically fit enough to go through with it.'

There was one concession to us as probationers; we got an afternoon off a week to be pumped full of the latest Inner London Education Authority (that's ILEA) directives and to compare notes from the trenches with the infantry in other schools. Besides giving us a tenth of our week 'off', ILEA looked after us in other ways; it supplied advisors, and the maths ones were Charlie and Bill.

Charlie and I formed a bond immediately; he would turn up in his red MG, bound into my school and surround me with positivity. He just loved working with young people, and they sensed immediately that here was someone they could trust completely. Bill, on the other hand, had not a clue what to make of me. As he saw it, I'd been to a nobby school and even nobbier university and he couldn't work out why I'd chosen the East End of London to ply my trade. In discussion once, a senior teacher said it'd taken two hundred hours to prepare a module of work, and I questioned why it'd taken that long. Bill's response was to stand and leave; this was arrogance that couldn't be tolerated, but apparently couldn't be directly challenged either.

Maybe I did come across as arrogant. Curiously, the nickname that my kids had already come up with for me was 'Lofty', a reference to my startling resemblance to the Eastenders character of that name. My friends thought this hilarious, one half urging me to squash the phenomenon, and the other half urging me to encourage it. But I've just read now what Wikipedia has to say about him;

Lofty is generally depicted as a meek and hapless victim.

Were my students making some kind of prediction?

Autographs

Stringfellow was only one of my indiscretions pre-teaching. I misspent my youth sufficiently to pack in an entire if brief musical career before picking up my whiteboard pen. Post-university, I forgot about education completely to pursue vague dreams in a band.

I took a risk here, but how big was it? Those were the days when student tuition fees were a grant; I left university owing nothing. The band (called *Harvey and the Wallbangers*) formed in my final year, and we'd seen enough thumbs raised by our audiences to realise we were onto something. For some of my colleagues, this was serious; they were aiming to be career musicians, and this was their stepping stone. Deep down, I still wanted to be a teacher, but I was curious as to how far the band might go. Maybe I'd learn skills that would one day improve my classroom technique?

Being sensible, I chose to pick up first the necessary bits of paper to make me at least look like a maths teacher. When those pesky band dreams didn't work out (and really, I'd always guessed they wouldn't) I was able to sigh, dust off my Department of Education teacher number and go straight out to buy a *Times Educational Supplement*.

Twenty years later, I'm sitting at a table on an Open Evening, writing some notes. A young colleague called Vera walks past, someone fresh to the college and not yet up to speed with the shared knowledge staff all have about each other, information that wraps every one of us in an invisible cloak. She says, 'You look as if you're writing autographs, Jonny!' and then laughs like a jackdaw.

I think back to performing at one music festival in Sweden, where we signed autographs for an hour after our set. Vera knows nothing about that; all she sees is a balding, tubby maths teacher who's nearing retirement scribbling away on a table.

'In 100 years time they might be worth something!' I reply with a smile. She cackles again as she walks away. Funny old world.

Grandparents

Today's starting problem with my first-year-of-A-Level class is on sequences. I look at the question as it shimmers on the whiteboard:

Grandma gives Henry £5 on his third birthday, and then increases this amount by £2 for each subsequent birthday. How much in total has he received by his tenth birthday?

This looks all right, I think, and my thoughts run obediently along the lines prescribed by the setter. *This is about arithmetic sequences (they're the ones that go up or down by a steady jump each time you move along one term) and the examiner has picked a family member as a convenient peg to hang this problem upon.*

But what are my students thinking, as they get to work on the problem in pairs and threes? As I survey the room, I can see little immediate appreciation of the mathematics of the situation. The word that has leapt out at my young charges is…

Grandma.

For each of my students, that word is now resonating, summoning up pictures of their own grandmothers and others, large and small.

How does the Grandma of the problem compare with their own? Her rule seems to speak of financial fidelity, of an increasing monetary commitment happily taken on, mirroring perhaps her growing love for her grandchild. Had any of my students' grandmothers been as explicit in the unwavering nature of their future generosity? Maybe in real life

47

there are invisible strings attached to birthday gifts, and by giving just one year at a time, conditions are silently put in place over what might or might not happen next year.

I call the class together to discuss their thoughts, and we move on to the next bit of the question together.

Grandpa gives Henry £5 on his first birthday, and then increases this amount by 10% for each subsequent birthday.

Rachel gasps. 'So he gets one present from his Grandma and another from his Grandpa!'

The human aspect of this tale begins to take over. Have Grandma and Grandpa conferred about their gifts? Does the separateness of their giving reflect some deeper division in their union? Do they even live together? A ripple of concern for the pair travels through the room.

Once the first few terms of Grandpa's giving are calculated, it's agreed he's a bit odd.

£5, £5.50, £6.05, £6.66, £7.32…

'So if I say, "I've seen a scarf for £7.33 that I really like, Grandpa," ' says Emily, 'then he'll say, "Sorry, you are only getting £7.32. I have a system, you know!" '

'That's what you get for having a grandparent who's a maths teacher,' mutters Lewis darkly.

'And for Christmas, Henry,' says Teala, putting on a pompous voice, 'you'll be getting a radian pounds!'

The discussion is making me uncomfortable. How did my own grandparents negotiate gifts on birthdays? My grandfather Gordon was a deeply precise man, who announced to all his grandchildren when I was ten that he'd placed £100 for each of us into a Post Office Savings Account, and that from now on we should buy our own birthday present each year by withdrawing the year's interest on the £100 ourselves on the appropriate date. The idea stuck me as efficient if unromantic – my gift from Grandfather Gordon would from now on be both entirely predictable and also something of an administrative chore, for me, if not for him.

'Did you go along with it?' ask my class, curious after I'd shared this tale.

'I took the whole lot out in one go and put it towards a bicycle,' I reply ruefully.

'Ah!' says Johnny, 'Bet you regret that now.'

'Did your Grandpa find out?' askes Gina, alarmed. 'Or did you keep that secret from him?'

This is becoming more akin to a psychotherapy session than a maths lesson. I do my best to drag the class back to the next part of the question.

On which birthday does the amount received by Henry from Grandma first exceed £50?

The answer turns out to be the 26th.

'Lucky bloke!' says Daniel, shocked. 'My grandparents gave up on giving me a birthday present when I was 15.'

We examine the notion (via a spreadsheet) that Grandma and Grandpa's rules might eventually turn into a real burden for them.

'If these rules last fifty-three years, that's over £10 000 between them,' says Mark.

'That's only going to happen,' says Amy, 'if Henry's mum and her mum were both teenage mothers.'

'Grandma, you slag!' says Martha unhelpfully.

So what to conclude from this? Firstly, I've always found that however much a question-writer tries to channel thinking down a particular river course, students will always find a way to burst its banks and head elsewhere, replacing abstraction with informality as they go.

Secondly, I'm all for really real-life problems appearing in classrooms, but does the above question qualify? Can we produce actual grandparents that behave in this bizarre fashion? The pretence that this fake version of 'real' life can be crowbarred into our sequences study eventually fades away. If the lesson above is anything to go by, could it fade away a little earlier?

Look the Part

My dress sense around the time I began life as a maths teacher in Tower Hamlets might best be described as charity shop chic. At university and in the band I'd amassed an array of fifties jackets that'd served me well, and I innocently thought my new protégés in Tower Hamlets would be impressed by my stylish brand of retro cool. How wrong can you be. My pupils fell silent as I walked in, before sharing a communal 'Ouch!' and finishing with shouts of 'Oxfam, was it, sir?' A student called Mavis took me on one side in a motherly way at the end of the lesson.

'Give yourself a treat, sir,' she said. 'Go to a proper shop and buy yourself something really nice.'

'What should I wear?' is a question that (almost) every mathematics teacher has to grapple with (presumably naturists need to learn maths too). Should one try to be impeccably smart, or is that a losing battle? Is mufti okay? Ties? Heels? Every teacher has their own more or less conscious take on the issue, and that take will be clearly visible to everyone else.

There are what I would call 'class implications' for one's couture. If you're aiming for promotion from the classroom to management, then you put on a suit. Mrs G's Law is that the height of a female teacher's heels is proportional to the loftiness of their position in the school hierarchy. On the other hand, there's a certain brand of mufti-wearing classroom teacher that's annoyed by colleagues' ties, and incensed at their waistcoats. David, my Head of Department, was in this group, and I sometimes wore the full outfit just to see him spit. Although I also think my get-up supplied a little distance between me and my classes, which is undeniably part of the job.

51

I don't often watch thrillers, but when I do, I've been known to nod off and experience a dream where I'm given the perfect clothing in which to teach maths.

Q, the greying Head of MI6, eyed up the two men.

'Jonny, I'd like you meet Dr Leonard Hoffstein – he's been working on an ingenious new Maths Suit for your next assignment. It comes, of course, with a full range of accessories.'

Jonny, slim and tanned after a week lecturing in California, smiled broadly as he shook Dr Hoffstein's hand.

'Delighted to meet you, Dr Hoffstein. The name's Gee. Jonny Gee. Licensed to teach mathematics.'

'Would you like to try your suit on, Mr Gee?' said Dr Hoffstein in flawless English. A few minutes later, Gee looked at himself in the mirror. The fit was perfect.

Looking more closely, he saw his suit was covered in carefully tailored pockets. There was a semi–circular one containing a protractor, a right–angled pair for a setsquare, and a neat 12–inch by 1–inch one where a metal ruler could be neatly secreted. Gee sighed with satisfaction and checked his TI–84 calculator carefully before slipping it smoothly into the under–arm holster.

Q and Dr Hoffstein purred over their sartorial creation.

'Now to explain a few little extras,' said Dr Hoffstein. 'These soft leather patches on the elbows are actually detachable mini–frisbees, excellent for giving someone in the back row a gentle wake up call.'

'Your left cufflink,' explained Q, 'is a laser pointer when pressed, while your right moves your Powerpoint on by one slide.'

Dr Hoffstein reached into one of Gee's hip pockets, withdrawing what looked like a fun-sized Milky Way.

'This may look like an ordinary chocolate bar, Jonny, but if you award it as a prize, it will administer a dose of Ritalin sufficient to sedate a rowdy student of average build for an entire 90–minute lesson.'

'Good luck, Gee,' said Q. 'You have a tough assignment ahead. InSpectre, as you know, is committed to making life miserable for us all…'

Of course, neither Q nor Dr Hoffstein nor anyone like them ever knocked on my door. Instead I stuck to my risk-free rules for teacher kit: nothing too flash, nothing too staid, and above all, everything built to last. And if I chanced across a virgin suit in a charity shop that fitted beautifully, one that everyone would assume was new, then - why not?

Spoiled for Choice

It's break–time. Some repair work is going on in the corner of the staffroom; there's been a problem with damp there for a while, and the powers that be have been slow to address it. As a protest, James, our Biology teacher, has attempted to grow cress on the rotting floor, and his crop was looking healthy when discovered by management. James remained cheerful whilst being berated by his superiors, but that was yesterday, and the damp is being dealt with today. His protest, it seems, was not in vain.

Andrea and I are discussing our Application of Number Level Two groups, and the multiple choice exam they will shortly be taking.

'How can I approach this exam without discussing strategy?' asks Andrea, bewildered. 'What if they can't do a question? I have to tell them to use their common sense, put a line through the crazy answers to improve their chances, and then take a guess. Ninety per cent of these questions then become an estimation exercise.'

I nod. Multiple choice papers vary. This one poses forty questions in an hour, each offering four choices, with no penalty for wrong answers. Thus random guessing means you will pick up 25% on average. If you know half the questions for sure and guess randomly on the rest, you get 62.5% on average. The pass mark is 55%.

As multiple choice papers go, I reckon this is pretty crude. Let me suggest a tweak; awarding 3 marks for a correct answer and taking 1 mark off for every wrong answer, which hopefully cuts out the incentive for random guessing. I could go further; there are MC papers out there that are mathematical works of art. Which combination of

54

these three facts is true, how are these statements logically connected, which of these bits of information is redundant, which combination of these facts in necessary to solve the problem; all these questions request insight, and they suit the multiple choice format perfectly. I am duty-bound to add that a good MC test is additionally the teacher's friend since it can be marked by a machine, and from the point of view of your workload gives you an assessment, however flawed, for free.

We both take further gulps of tea as our ridiculously short break–time comes to an end.

'I'm not saying that passing on a multiple choice exam means nothing,' I say. 'I know that being able to estimate sensibly is a hugely valuable skill, it's just that…'

I wrinkled my nose, and Andrea nodded.

'Teaching like this makes me feel ashamed,' she confesses through sips of black tea (milk tends to be a battleground issue in our staffroom). 'Dirty, even.'

We move through to the kitchen to sluice out our mugs. Passing a Level Two qualification in maths is given grail–like importance for students who don't have such a thing, and yet we often hear of the disappointment employers feel.

'Why,' they ask, 'does this qualification turn out to represent so little?'

I sigh as I wipe. 'The answer could be A….'

Supply and demand

Teaching at St Philip Howard meant swiftly understanding the concept of a supply teacher. Simply, a supply teacher covers for missing colleagues. Francis is off ill, or John has a course, and Heather comes in to take their lessons for the day. The alternative? That regular teachers give up their free lessons to cover, which is understandably fantastically unpopular (after all, this penalises those who come in faithfully). I once heard of a teacher who would count up cover lessons until they'd been given six to do and then, despite being in perfect health, take a day off – 'It's only fair.' Selfish, possibly, but maybe it's only the teachers with a streak of selfishness who tend to survive.

Supply teachers generally plan no work and mark no work; most get in later than regular teachers and leave long before them. The down side is that they're often (but far from always) regarded as clownish strangers by their classes, who are probably deep down miffed that their real teacher isn't there and behave accordingly. There's also the problem that the teachers they are replacing may have left work that is not so much thin as ten denier. I know of one music teacher who 'planned' the six lessons he would be missing, all for different year groups, with the single phrase, 'My dear boy, I think you'll find something helpful in the piano stool.' You could hardly blame a supply teacher in such a situation for saying, 'I'm going to give you each a score of Beethoven's Fifth, and I'd like you colour it in.'

One way of assessing a school is to ask how many full-time supply teachers they employ. A good school might manage with a few part-timers most of the time. St Philip Howard had maybe eight full-time supply teachers (and this was not a big school) who came in all day, every day. It was just expected that people would be off. My brother

Richard, an assistant head, reports of one day where thirty different teachers in his 'demanding' school required at least one lesson to be covered in the course of a single day.

At St Philip Howard, these supply specialists varied hugely in attitude and ability. I recall Anita, a hugely talented Australian working in supply to earn a bit of cash before 'doing' Europe. She would walk into a classroom like a gunslinger entering a bar full of beardy ne're-do-wells, and leave her pupils open-mouthed with the speed of her delivery. They had no idea what had hit them.

The contrast with Edward could not have been greater. He was beyond retirement age; there had to be some tragic reason for the fact he was still trying his luck as a supply teacher in a difficult school. Maybe he was an out-of-work actor filling his time with what was for him a relatively well-paid job. He always seemed to be wearing the same tie encrusted with the same flecks of food. There was a rumour that somewhere within the school each night he found a desk to kip behind. I once walked into a lesson he was 'taking' to find him reading a book while the pupils treated the room as a playground.

The most appalling thing about Edward was his complete lack of self-respect. One day I saw him walking towards me along a corridor. I watched a student pass him, lift his hand and casually ruffle Edward's hair. Edward just kept walking. I'd never seen anything so demeaning in my life; a student throwing a chair at you would be infinitely preferable. *Please God,* I prayed as I walked past Edward myself, *if it ever comes to that, someone just shoot me.*

Young Beautiful Minds

It's unusual that I fail to get to the end of a television programme about mathematics. Such an event is rare enough, so I would anticipate it, booking my place on the sofa ahead of any rival claims from Mrs G, arguing there's a Marple she just HAS to watch. Yet this programme, a study of those preparing for the International Maths Olympiad, left me feeling so bereft that I switched off early. What was it that threw me so badly?

We were introduced to the Olympiad hopefuls, all young, all extraordinary, and almost all male. Extraordinary in their abilities, but undeniably disabled too (maybe that goes for all of us). Some, like Josh, had been diagnosed as autistic, but several others could have been placed towards that end of the spectrum. Some were grappling with their identity, painfully and openly; nowhere did there seem to be an easy relationship with the world of other people. Mathematics became for these often unhappy young souls a release and a haven, and as I watched, I became grateful that they were here being given at least one such refuge.

What angle did the director (Morgan Matthews) choose to take? Dispassionate observation; yet is there any such thing? All 'facts' are theory–laden. As these socially dysfunctional but mathematically hyper–functional young people were interviewed, I felt increasingly uneasy, as though they were being set up, and as if something I cherished was being trashed along the way.

Was Matthews a mathematician? Had he ever experienced any joy from mathematical thinking, joy that these young people undeniably felt? It seemed unlikely. On show was an underlying horror of how these mathematicians and the people who taught them viewed the world.

Was this the terrible lesson of this film – that mathematics can draw bright awkward children in and fill them with a sense of worth that they find hard to experience with other people, yet the more that respite is sought in mathematics, the more bonds of kinship with others are ignored, and from there the only replacement for those fading relationships is to spend more time with mathematics. Mathematics as a drug that deadens the pain of trying to relate to people. Mathematics as disability, despite being brilliant at it.

Maybe there was nothing special about mathematics in all this. The same film could have been made about obsessives who spend unhealthy tracts of their time on Scrabble, chess or poetry. As people surrender balance in their lives, so they become documentary fodder, whatever their fix in life. But even so, it still hurt to watch.

No, I didn't make it to the end of the programme. Maybe there was some redemption, some lightening of the atmosphere. But the next day I ran into Ralph, a colleague who teaches solely on the Arts side of the College. I would say Ralph harbours a more or less explicit philosophy that mathematics is for emotional inadequates. He smiled gleefully as he discussed the film with me. He didn't quite say, 'It's what I've been thinking for years,' but he might as well have done.

I quoted young Arthur to him. 'Discos try to blind you and deafen you simultaneously. If I wanted to be both blind and deaf, I'd go into a cave of sleeping bats, and wake them up.'

Ralph's cackling echoed down the corridor as he walked away.

Week Two

I made it through month one in Tower Hamlets somehow. St Philip Howard had bigger fish to fry, I was discovering, than the travails of a rookie maths teacher who was wetter behind the ears than a baby elephant having a shower. But I'd landed on my feet in one sense at least; my frighteningly young Head of Department, Margaret Davison, was a magician. She'd been at the school herself as a young student, and she knew the culture inside out. Having her on my side was decidedly a plus.

I decided one day to try to model my disciplinary persona on that of a football referee. I bought a notebook, and at the first sign of trouble, I whipped it out and noted down the misdemeanour and the perpetrator. On its first appearance, my book enjoyed an impressive if mystified silence. When called upon a second time, its aura had decidedly diminished, and by the end of the lesson, it held little fear for anyone. When my notebook emerged in the following lesson with that group, I watched Matt draw an almost identical book from his jacket pocket and make notes furiously in time with me. I sighed.

Wandering the corridors during a free period was an education. The sound emanating from most rooms was that of 'lively' work; certainly I wasn't the only teacher fighting to keep order. But walk past Margaret's room, and the sound dropped to zero. Walk in, and one felt the blast from the work-furnace taking place within its walls.

One morning I was battling to keep my young protégés on task. Had I set something beyond them, something inappropriate? There were certainly complaints of, 'This is boring!', and they were getting louder.

My vertigo was hitting unacceptable levels. And then, the blessed Margaret was at my door.

She stood in silence. The pupils one by one noticed, and the magic happened. They stopped throwing paper and nicking pens and chewing gum and looking out of the window and jostling each other and just... settled. A near-silence descended, a gentle hum of work began, and material that had been incomprehensible became accessible, whilst most miraculously of all, questions that had been boring became interesting.

Margaret handed me a document with a smile, and left the room. She'd not said a word. Gradually paradise unravelled; someone coughed, someone dropped a pen on the floor, someone whispered, someone laughed, another laugh from over here, someone put their hand up, saying 'I don't get this!', and my chaotic square one was rapidly revisited.

That break-time, I mulled this over as I peered at the trees outside, struggling bravely up through the concrete. How did she do it? Was it a set of techniques that I could learn? Or was it a God-given gift that lesser mortals who'd not been honoured in this way would never have?

Christina, another teacher in our maths department who admired Margaret, laughed when I raised this with her at the end of the day.

'Here's one technique for you, Jonny. A kid drops a bit of litter. Do you say, "Joe, pick that up!"? Or do you say first, "Joe, could you please put that in the bin?" If he does what you ask, you win. If he ignores you, follow up with, "Joe! In the bin! Now!" Ask, then tell. That's what my mum used to say, bless her.'

I tried Christina's tip out the next day; it helped. But could I learn enough of these teacher-wrinkles before I collapsed in a heap with exhaustion? My graph of Sanity against Technical Ability against Time did not look good.

Margaret herself was philosophical. 'We've all been through it, Jonny. Just wait until your second year. You'll have become part of the furniture.'

But then I watched Margaret enter her classroom. It already held a full class, and she paused as she held the door-handle. I could see her take a second to put on her armour, and I heard a small intake of breath. Yes, she had amazing control over her classes, but that certainly came at a cost.

Scrap

I'm building a cube for my next lesson. It's getting there, but my twelve edges need to be strengthened. I reach for some scrap paper. Out of curiosity, I flip the sheet to see what's on the typed side.

Ofsted Report on Paston College

The strengths of the mathematics department are these…

Close, but no cigar

It's the Christmas quiz in my classroom.

Me: Who wrote *War and Peace*?

Team leader (after long discussion): Was it Trotsky?

Me: No, sorry, it was Tolstoy.

Pause.

Team leader: Can we have half a mark?

Jazz-Time

Mrs G whispers into my ear. 'He's about to start writing on windows...'

We're sitting in the cinema watching a film providing yet one more take on the theme of unstable mathematical genius. The movie, *Proof*, which is turning out to be excellent, goes one better than most in having <u>two</u> of these maverick characters, with the father and the daughter vying for the accolade of Most Convincing Algebraic Oddball.

The girl's talking to her supervisor. She's wandered off the point in her differential equations assignment and has started to improvise, putting down original maths that really means something to her. Her professor leafs through her work with disdain before pronouncing, 'Mathematics is not jazz!' (His remark draws an appreciative chuckle from my better half.)

As the screen flickers, I think of both my mathematical education and my musical one. At school, I was introduced to music classically, a whirl of choirs and orchestras and manuscript paper. Music was something platonic, technique was everything, and mistakes were ugly and to be regretted. I learnt to associate a dot on a page with a physical action to produce a sound, effectively bypassing my ears in the process. Progress meant tackling an ever–ascending series of exams, with the implicit message that your version of a classic piece would never be worth much of a listen when compared with that of a virtuoso. I grew up loving classical music, but fearing it too.

Mrs G snuggles up, taking my arm while chewing mechanically on a pastille. It appears this girl has come up with some maths that really does break new ground, but it is obvious from her muffled snort that that Mrs G remains to be impressed.

Then one day, I heard the strains of Dave Brubeck's *Take Five*. I was hooked. I devoured the jazz albums my local library had to offer. I changed the way I played the violin, towards improvising on different themes in ways that reflected my personality, where any 'wrong' note was not shunned, but repeated with pleasure until it turned into a 'right' one.

I formed a jazz quartet where we listened to each other, responding to our mutual promptings in ways that added an immediacy to what we were doing. No performance was just like any other, and every performance we gave could only have been ours.

I still love classical music, I reflect, and classical technique is useful to me whatever I'm playing. But I don't want to teach maths classically, at least, not all the time. I want my students to be able to improvise on a mathematical theme, to enjoy their mathematical uniqueness, and not to fear mistakes but to be thankful for them, and learn from them.

My partner shifts a little in her seat. Her prediction about windows has proved to be almost correct; I watch the girl's father covering the pages of his notebook with mad mathematical nonsense.

'What are you thinking, love?' she whispers.

'I'm just thinking that real maths IS jazz, actually…'

Mathematicians are from Mars

Today I've reached the part of the course for first–year A Level mathematicians that I love the most; proof. Unique to maths, the business of how we attempt to establish things with complete, eternal certainty always fills me with awe. I'm opening up with one of my favourite gambits by introducing a Martian into our reflections, someone who knows nothing of what the human race has achieved mathematically down the years.

'So you all know Pythagoras's Theorem, good,' I say. 'But do you know how to prove it? Suppose a Martian came down to visit, who'd never seen Pythagoras's Theorem before; how would you convince them it was always true?'

I get a raised hand from Chelsea, an over-earnest sci-fi fan in the back row. She speaks in complete seriousness.

'Don't you think there's a danger, Jonny, that if we share our mathematics with aliens they will take it and use it against us?'

Once the lesson's back on track (several minutes of shared laughter later), I find a moment to reflect on Chelsea's vision. Would Martians take as blindingly obvious things of which we've never conceived? Would their mathematics emphasize things we take as trivial, if we have noticed them at all? And above all, would this mathematics be easier for my students to learn? Would it be, in any sense, closer to 'true' mathematics?

Our maths is still incredibly Greek. At around 300 BC the world welcomed an Alexandrian mathematician called Euclid, who reorganised mathematics in a startling way by assuming a few simple statements (axioms) and building more complicated ones from them (theorems). Mathematicians on Earth still take Euclid's view of the world as the natural way to operate, although it might not be so for the Martians. It would not have taken much to tweak our vision in a different direction. If instead of drawing lines on the sand, Euclid had spent his time looking at shadows on a wall, our geometry textbooks might now instead tackle the subject in a way that appears odd to us.

I look around the room, as my students battle away with proof problems. Maybe when they find things hard, and ask difficult, even offbeat, questions, they're groping their way towards Martian mathematics.

One day, I think, *might one of you actually discover it, making all of our lives that much easier?*

Snowy day

There are teacher slips, there are teacher errors, and then there are teacher howlers. However long you've been teaching, you'll commit all three of these regularly. Take me the other day.

'That's the syllabus done,' I say triumphantly, 'and we're into revision now - so how can I help you? For the rest of the lesson, I'd like you all to regard me as your slave.'

My students confer urgently for three minutes. I've not seen this intensity of group work for a while. Eventually their spokesperson Natasha announces their verdict.

'We'd like you to dance like a monkey.'

In case I'd not understood my assignment, I'm shown a video on someone's phone of, well, men in monkey-suits dancing. I draw myself up to my full height, summon up as much dignity as I can, and refuse.

There may be some people out there who say that in the classroom, a maths teacher should talk about maths and nothing else. It's true that some students love to explore a red herring at the expense of learning, and that such a ruse needs to be dispatched with gentle humour. But you cannot expect young adults to have no curiosity at all about those teaching them. One day I was asked by a group what I thought about gay sex. There was a lad called Stan in the class who was being bullied on account of his orientation, and they knew I called myself a Christian. I said that I thought that if two people loved each other, and had entered into a life commitment together, then regardless of gender, to express that physically was tickety-boo. The class seemed satisfied. The idea

68

that I should refuse to answer the question and insist that we grind on with vectors seems inhuman to me.

Big mistake number two. It's a snowy day, but not an extremely snowy day, which would be known as A Snow Day, where teachers around the county awaken with a song in their heart as they pull back the curtains and hear the radio tell them their school is closed. Today I've half a class, those whose parents have booted them out into the cold and ignored cries of, 'It's not worth going in, I tell you!' This A Level half-group before me now is finding it hard to concentrate, as five girls on the lawn below are spelling out a word by rolling a big snowball across the grass.

'What does that say?' asks Martin, peering at their handiwork down on the lawn. The others give up on their work, and eagerly gather around the window.

I sigh. With so many snow casualties, this lesson was wrecked at the start, and now it seems the maths is being upstaged further by the snow-sculptors down below. I decide that remonstrations are pointless, and that my only sensible course of action is to join in with the enquiry.

We squint at the green tracks that divide up the white covering.

'Is that the word, "Queer"?' asks Anne in disbelief. An unhelpful choice, if that's the case, although I gather the word is currently being reclaimed by some.

'No, that last letter is definitely an F,' says Dave. This has turned into a decoding exercise now, and the whole class, myself included, wants to see the riddle cracked.

Eventually we agree the word is, definitely, 'Queef.'

'What does that mean?' asks Anne, still bemused. Nobody knows.

'Google it!' the class says as one. The girls outside are left to their project, and everyone in the room is now focused on the board, where a copy of my computer screen sits obligingly.

Overriding my teacher intuitions, all of which are busily shouting 'Danger!', I find that a site called The Urban Dictionary is willing to supply insight. I decide to make this theatrical.

'And so, ladies and gentlemen, the word "Queef" means…,' I say extravagantly, as I press the mouse. I'm as much in the dark as anyone else. The definition hangs on the board, and there is a stunned silence.

It's Paul who speaks first, and he could not sound more matter-of-fact.

'It's "a vaginal fart".'

A sudden depression descends upon my soul. *What the hell is one of those?* My life, which suddenly appears to be worryingly sheltered, flashes before my eyes. The implications unravel. I hear a parent asking one of my students over dinner, 'What did you do in maths today?' Then I see the Daily Mail headline;

'Queefs are on maths syllabus,' claims rogue teacher.

Have I dishonoured my female students with my stupidity? I look round to find to my relief that the girls are laughing at least as heartily as the

70

boys. Martin goes back over to the window, and lifts it up, as the rest of the class claps and cheers.

'Hey, respect!' he shouts to the quintet of girls below.

Maybe it'll be all right. I look out of the window, and I can see that the girls have moved onto a new project.

'It's a snowman,' I think, relieved. But then, looking more closely, it seems to be quite erect… oh dear…

You Surprise Me

Here's a short conversation I overheard not long ago at a maths education conference:

Delegate A: Which session are you going to next?
Delegate B: I'm going to the one on 'Surprise'.
Delegate A: Oh.

In maths ed journals, many of which are currently piled up on my desk in dusty heaps, surprise is always presented as the Ingredient X, the pedagogical Viagra that every teacher need to add to their lessons to enthral students and revolutionise learning.

There's a lot of truth in this. An example which many maths teachers will know: take almost any three-digit number (the only ones not allowed are those whose first and final digits differ by 1 or 0). Let's say we pick

472.

Now write your number backwards, and take the smaller from the larger, giving

472 - 274 = 198.

Now write this number backwards, and ADD it to the other, so

198 + 891 = 1089.

The surprise? You always get 1089, whatever number you start with. Try it!

This is always a hit with students, and it ushers in the natural question, can we PROVE this always works? As a springboard into the power of algebra, it's hard to better this example.

But a subversive thought occurs to me (I see it my job as Chief Heretic to play Devil's Advocate at every opportunity). 'Could surprise become so pervasive a strategy in the maths classroom that it becomes mundane?'

As I look around my class, I see students who find A Level maths hard. Let's imagine a post-lesson conversation with a typical such student Camilla.

'Camilla, your test score was down? How do you feel about your maths at the moment?'

'I'm just not getting it. The others all get it.' She looks annoyed.

'Can I ask, when you chose your A levels, why did you pick maths?'

'I wanted a challenge. Mum and Dad said maths is a proper A Level. "It'll help you get a job!" they said. "It looks good on a CV." And in any case, I'm doing Physics and Chemistry, so I have to do maths, to back them up.'

'How did maths go for you at High School?'

'I didn't get an A* or anything, but my teacher said I could take it on to A Level. But maths was much easier then…'

'Camilla, can you name one bit of maths that you've really enjoyed? That you really thought was neat? Not just from this year, but ever?'

Camilla furrows her brow. 'No. Maths has never been like that for me. Ever.'

With all these competing motives and thoughts fighting it out in her psyche, Camilla sits in my class and tries to understand the subject.

Maybe the problem here is less 'not enough surprise' as 'too much surprise'. Camilla experiences wave after wave of novelty each lesson, as the number of areas where she fails to understand grows, and gallingly, she sits next to students who do understand, effortlessly, as it appears to her, who greet yesterday's formula as an old friend and who never seem to forget anything.

'If you don't understand, please, ask,' I invite. 'There's no such thing as a foolish question in this class.'

Yet Camilla doesn't believe me, as next lesson she struggles to construct a query that will not betray her complete at–sea–ness in too embarrassing a way. While she's battling to do this, she's missing the point of the next piece of mathematics, and so it goes on.

We go to see a magic show to be surprised. 'How does he do that?' But such a show assumes that we're comfortable with what happens in everyday life when we saw a wardrobe in half, when we try to walk on water, or when we pick a secret card. In a world with no reliability over

74

these things, there's no surprise when something unpredictable happens, and no one enjoys magic.

I look up from my musings, and glance around. I can see the mathematics education community looking solemn, as they draw up excommunication documents. I decide to pull back from the brink.

'Yes, let's have surprise in the maths classroom,' I say to my judges, 'but let's use it to create gentle shocks, where the surprise of seeing one's mathematics challenged or affirmed is an enjoyable growing point.'

Can I see my colleagues look more approving? 'I would say that to welcome surprise,' I add, emboldened, 'you need to have a secure framework in place, that's ready to be challenged, and you need to trust that the delicious resolution of that surprise will actually take place, making your framework stronger in the process.'

As I now look across at Camilla, I ask, 'Can you come to actually value this feeling of at–sea–ness?'

Camilla quietly replies, 'Yes, if you give me the confidence that whenever I feel that way, I'll always move on to a sense of land–ahoy–ness.'

Leroy

Week five, and St Philip Howard was being kinder to me, but not by much. I would swing wildly between believing that I'd cracked it, to a day of despair, when all hint of control deserted me.

One day I tore my hair out over a class that was rowdier than hell itself. Margaret offered her help.

'At your next lesson with this crowd, which is tomorrow, line them up outside before letting them in. Read them the riot act. I'll come along and support you.'

So that's what happened. I had the twenty-five students in a line snaking off down the corridor, and I did my best to administer a telling-off.

'I was truly shocked, 3 Gwyn, at your behaviour last lesson!' I said.

Leroy, a languid boy with sharp eyes, put up his hand.

'I wasn't here last lesson,' he said, with a humour-laden smugness.

This was true. I flailed mentally, searching for that magic put-down.

'Well – well, if you HAD been, Leroy, you would've been as shocked as I was!'

Leroy took in what I'd said, and smirked. Pockets of laughter broke out down the line. I turned to see a despairing Margaret.

This was most definitely not how she would have done it. When I watched her talk to a difficult student, I could see all possible conversations branching out into a huge tree, and at the end of every final twig were the two words, 'Margaret wins.' Every student she talked to could sense that tree, and the futility of trying to triumph in the game.

My tree had plenty of twigs that ended in the leaf, 'Student wins'. They would eagerly take me on, knowing their chance of success were good.

Leroy wasn't that interested in maths as I tried to convey it to him, but his facility in related areas was remarkable. He would pull out a Rubik's cube and solve it in seconds, his fingers flashing the colours into position like a kingfisher diving in the sun.

'That's amazing,' I thought, as I watched him show off to his fellow learners at the end of the lesson. 'But the techniques I'm asking you to learn, Leroy are, I promise you, profounder than manipulating the colours on a cube.'

As the group broke up with whoops of admiration over Leroy's performance, I shook my head in sadness. 'So why can't I get you to show the same ambition with the skills I'm offering you?'

I'd like you to Q, PDQ!

As with every walk of life, mathematics teaching has its gurus. One of these is John Holt, writer of the seminal book *How Children Fail*. Within its pages, he tells the story of how he one day invented the Q.

'When I wanted quiet I would write a capital Q in a corner of the blackboard, with the rule:

When the Q is on the board, there shall be no talking except by those who have raised their hand and have had permission.'

He describes the response invented by his pupils to accompany his new ritual.

'When I began to write the Q, they would all make a murmur, rising to a shriek as I boxed in the Q with a flourish. But as soon as my chalk hit the edge of the blackboard, dead silence.'

I must confess my own hand-written Q was always regarded as idiosyncratic by my students.

'Please, Jonny, add the sombrero! Pleeeze!'

That aside, the John Holt story above shows that an abbreviation can be far more powerful than the whole word, and a ritual can be far stronger than the individual actions that make it up. I too realised one day while teaching a GCSE resit group that I didn't want to win silence by shouting the class down. I wrote an S in a circle on the overhead projector, and waited. Most of the class cottoned on fast, eventually leaving the loudest kid in the group saying, 'So why has he written an S on the board? Why has he...' The silence that resulted was especially delicious.

I swiftly expanded my range of abbreviations. TM stood for Talk–Maths (you can talk about maths but nothing else), J stood for Jonny–Time (whole class discussion directed by me) and B stood for break (no reasonable topic off limits for discussion.) I was establishing different modes of operation, each with their own rules, and I gradually sorted out what I could reasonably expect from my students within each mode. If my class would not TM, then no B. I even used the abbreviation SMB for Show Me Boards, plastic slates that could be easily wiped clean and which students loved using, until one day I asked one class what SMB might stand for, and Colin piped up, 'Sad mathematical bastard?'

When it comes to abbreviations, mathematics possesses one of the most famous of all time, the only entry Euclid has in my book of quotations, that is, QED. Quod Erat Demonstrandum – what was to be shown is shown. I remember the lesson in which I told the class how Euclid

79

would pronounce a statement proved with this three–letter flourish. But then Christine added, 'Shouldn't there be three letters for when you disprove a statement? With a counter–example?' We agreed that there should, and a mini–competition ensued. The joint winners were eventually IYD, for 'In Your Dreams,' and GOH, for 'Get Outta Here!'

Some abbreviations help, some don't. The topic of education seems to inspire people to flood the world with a bewildering array of initials, some as alienating as they are pointless. They can induce a fear within teachers. Last Inset day the Maths department were presented with a sheet of criteria for Application of Number, each with a little square alongside and the letters, M, E, T.

'What the hell does Em, Ee, Tee stand for?' asked Peter, in despair. 'Why does nobody tell me anything around here?'

'Peter, I think you'll find that Em, Ee, Tee is MET,' said a colleague quietly. 'You tick a box if one of the criteria has been met.'

I worked with one teacher who abbreviated 'students' to 'studs', which was surely asking for trouble. One set of department minutes included this; 'Homework. Some studs claimed they weren't getting enough.' Yes, but what about the homework?

Abbreviations exclude those who are not in the know, and sometimes this exclusivity can work to your advantage. I remember teaching a highly creative but motor–mouthed individual called Douglas who could easily get out of hand. I invented the abbreviation TLB for him: *The Library Beckons...*

Whenever Douglas's stream of consciousness became a torrent, TLB poured oil onto the waters. The knowledge that we in this class were the only people in the world who understood the meaning of TLB created a secret bond, a little frisson each time it was used.

It worked, on every occasion except one – what? I had to show him I meant it, surely?

Amy's Mistake

It's 10 pm, and I'm sitting at home in my study marking, with my ferocious angle-poise lamp doing its best to set my pile of scripts on fire. Sadly when my students had tackled this assignment, 'on fire' is something they'd decidedly not been. I throw back my head and yawn; three papers to go.

I turn to Amy's, and I come across this:

$$\frac{x^2}{x^2 - 9} = \frac{x}{x - 3}$$

I pause. This is not written down as an equation, which would be fine; its only solution would be x = 0. No, it's an attempt at simplifying the algebraic fraction on the left hand side, so this is a mistake. She's offering this as an identity, which would mean that the left-hand side is identically equal to the right-hand side for all values of x. She is in error; and how bad an error is this? Pretty bad, for an A2 student twelve weeks from her final exams. I wonder briefly if I should cover her page with gentle admonishments, but instead I try to do some unravelling.

What blooper has Amy actually made? She's saying for starters,

'If you do the same thing to the top and bottom of a fraction, its value is unchanged.'

Hmm. That's truish, I guess, some of the time. Now she takes the square root of top and bottom – is that allowed? I don't think so. There's the tempting sub–mistake now of saying

82

$$\sqrt{a^2 - b^2} = a - b,$$

which every maths teacher will have seen a zillion times. To explode this misconception, I can write this;

$$\sqrt{5^2 - 3^2} = 4 \neq 5 - 3.$$

So $\sqrt{a^2 - b^2} = a - b$ cannot be generally true.

The next lesson, with Amy's permission, I put her 'identity' on the board.

$$\frac{x^2}{x^2 - 9} = \frac{x}{x - 3}$$

'How could I show simply that this is not always true?' I ask.

Ronan sticks up a hand. 'Just try some numbers?'

'Good, Ronan. Let's put 4 in for x. The left hand side becomes $\frac{16}{7}$, while the right hand side is 4. We can safely say what Amy has written is not generally true.'

'But you've told us, Jonny,' pleads Amy, 'that if you do the same thing to the top and bottom of a fraction, its value is unchanged!'

'Amy, that's partly true. If you're multiplying top and bottom by something, or dividing by something, no problem. But if you're adding, or subtracting, or squaring, or as in this case, square rooting, there IS a problem.'

The class look uncomfortable.

83

'Look, is this always true?' I cry, writing on the board

$$\frac{a}{b} = \frac{\sqrt{a}}{\sqrt{b}}$$

'That's square rooting the top and the bottom, like you did Amy.'

I take a vote; a third say, 'True', two thirds say, 'False', abstaining is not allowed. Getting my students to commit engenders a welcome alertness around the room.

'This would mean,' I continue, 'that

$$a\sqrt{b} = b\sqrt{a}.$$

If a and b are non-zero, I can now divide by $\sqrt{a}\sqrt{b}$ to get

$\sqrt{a} = \sqrt{b}$ and so $a = b$.

So square-rooting the top and bottom of a fraction does not leave it unchanged except in this obvious special case.'

I'd hit the mark with this; everyone was looking happier.

'So Amy effectively suggested that $\frac{a^2}{b^2 - c^2} = \frac{a}{b - c}$. Can this ever be true? If we take this as an equation, rather than an identity, what then?'

84

The class sank into discussion, covering paper with working. After a few minutes, I bring things back together. Mary comes up to the board to write.

'Removing the fractions, we get
$$a^2(b - c) = a(b^2 - c^2),$$
she intones. 'Now we know that
$$b^2 - c^2 = (b + c)(b - c).$$
I nod approvingly. This factorisation is called 'the difference of two squares', which turns up at least three times in any sitting of exam papers, and which can be checked by multiplying out the right-hand side.

'So
$$a^2(b - c) = a(b - c)(b + c),$$
and we can divide by
$$a(b - c)$$
to get
$$a = b + c.$$

'As long as a is not zero, and b is not equal to c, because then we'd be dividing by zero, which is not allowed! Excellent, Mary – can you give an example of that working in practice?' I ask.

'So if, for example, c = 5, b = 6 and a = 11,' Mary continues, 'we have
$$\frac{11^2}{6^2 - 5^2} = \frac{11}{6 - 5}$$
which is true!'

We're all agreed; Amy's rule for simplification is wrong, but there are special cases when we can 'get away with it'.

So this mistake has been explored, hopefully without recrimination but with curiosity. As with most mistakes, there was something right about it, and Amy can take heart from that. It she'd been right first time, this helpful discussion would have been denied to us (I would say marking perfect scripts is less interesting for the teacher than tackling ones with the occasional mysterious error).

Is checking not a vital skill? Of course. Am I advocating deliberate mistakes? Of course not. Unless we're remarkable mathematicians, honest mistakes aplenty will come along of their own accord. Yes, we will try to make exams mistake-free zones, but it's only lapses that crop up beforehand that have a chance of being knocked on the head before the big day. And now the neuroscience tells us that brain size and activity actually increase when making a mistake; which doesn't happen when getting something right.

'Mistakes down the ages have sometimes been a big help,' I tell Amy's group before they go. 'I'm thinking of penicillin, or cornflakes, or the Post-It note. May our mathematical aberrations, God willing, be as fruitful as these.'

Racist Rap

Things in the East End two months in were still touch and go. Some of my lessons were fine if I listened to advice, set decent work, and held my more ridiculous ambitions in check. Other lessons were more about containment. But just over the horizon, the cavalry was about to arrive, in the shape of Smile.

Smile was a system of workcards devised jointly by mathematics teachers in 1980s London, a superlative communal effort. Smile back then became something of a maths teacher religion, and you could see why. The quality of the cards was self-evident, offering lively, practical experiences to students who'd not seen maths that way before. Each student was given their own list of cards to work through, a unique programme. The teacher, therefore, did not generally talk from the front of the class; you could well have four students on one table, all working on different things. A rowdy individual (who could single-handedly wreck a whole class lesson delivered from the board) could only disrupt their table, which was undesirable, but better than taking the whole class down with them. Meanwhile, the ambitious workers in the group could plough on, calling upon the teacher as a facilitator or librarian, rather than someone constantly trying to hold the attention of the entire group. Teaching the Smile way meant questioning the previously unquestioned, a genuine paradigm shift.

As a department, we'd decided to switch to Smile, and the day for the launch was the following week. In a meeting to plan this, my colleagues tried to perk me up after the lousy end I'd had to that particular day.

'Why don't you bring in some of your music?' said Helen in despair. 'They'd love that.'

I sighed. Suddenly, pushed into a corner and forced to think with immediacy in order to survive another day, I began to rap.

'Hey, today's the start of something new, it's a new kind of maths for me and you...'

My colleagues looked at each other, startled, before saying as one, 'That's it.'

Three days later I walked into my classroom holding a cassette player, and without saying a word, started a drum track. I was enjoying more attention than I'd received at any point thus far in my career. Mouths gaped silently as I gyrated before them.

'Yes, maths is cool, maths is fine, you can learn with me if you toe the line...'

There were some handy didactic points hidden within the text; for example, a key desire built into Smile was that students should learn from their mistakes.

'Don't let an error just slip by, if you've made a mistake, please understand why!'

Helen was right, my students loved it; I was forced to repeat *The Smile Rap* at the end of the lesson, and the news spread fast. Next day, all my other classes insisted I rap before they'd do anything. The word ran around the staffroom, ILEA got to hear, and thrill above all thrills, I duly received an invitation to perform at the Smile Conference, the legendary event where all the glitterati of the Smile movement gathered together for a maths-rich weekend.

The conference came, and I rapped the rap in my white tuxedo before handing out the words and getting the delegates to rap the rap too. Everyone (well, almost everyone) roared with laughter, and I soaked up the warm applause. Patting myself on the back, I headed for the bar, where the conference organizer came up looking shocked.

'Jonny, your rap - a number of people walked out,' he said abruptly.

Some teachers, both white and black, had been offended by my rendition. The accusation was that I'd 'misappropriated black culture.' Maybe I should have been devastated, but instead I smiled grimly.

'That's okay, the band I was in did that for years.'

The next day in a plenary, the organizer made an apology to the conference. But then, in a strange reversal, the teachers who'd enjoyed my performance were offended by the apology. One came up to me to express surprise, saying, 'I don't have any problem with what you did.' Others were angrier.

On the Monday I saw my students, from a rainbow of different heritages, who knew how my weekend had been planned. 'How did it go?' they asked eagerly. I didn't know what to say.

Keith, one of my colleagues in the band, was derisive when he heard the story. 'None of your critics, if they are being consistent, Jonny, should listen to any popular music written since 1911. Crossover is inevitable!'

Did the protesters in fact take me seriously? Did they think I had genuine ambitions as a rap artist? Could they not see that I was offering a pastiche, and that I'd never listened to a rap recording for pleasure in my life? Or maybe that was the problem? If I'd tried to be genuinely within the canon, honestly attempting to emulate the rap greats, then would that have been acceptable?

I wasn't entirely surprised by how things had unfolded. Playing in a band of white lads who'd admired black musicians whom they'd then covered, I'd run into this debate before. Should we only perform songs written and made famous by white artists? Are some genres 'black' and others 'white'? Is singing in an accent always offensive? Am I no longer allowed to sing 'Is you is or is you ain't my baby?' (because that's a lot of disappointed punters if so, let me tell you). Should I change it to 'Are you or are you not my significant other?' It doesn't sound quite the same.

A musical world where white musicians only sing songs by white musicians, and black singers stick to songs by black songwriters sounds profoundly unhealthy to me. Mad, even.

Looking back, I would say my performance was innocent but in part misguided. Cultural bad manners, perhaps. I hate racism, but I have blind spots, as we all do, and I was grateful (honest!) for having this one exposed. But it still hurts that no one who walked out had the mixture of compassion and balls to come and talk to me directly about what I'd done. In my book, that's a blind spot too.

Spectacles

My Paston second year students are immersed in their trig explorations. As I wander among them, I'm hit by a sudden realisation – when I talk to Suzanne and Ricky and Jane about their work, I'm looking at each of them over the top of my spectacles. How long have I been doing this? I have no idea, but I like it.

It is, of course, true that when you try to teach someone, steady and friendly eye contact is exceedingly desirable. The new question that suddenly faces me is, should I accomplish this through glass, or over glass?

I take off my spectacles, and give them a clean with a grubby hankie. These are not half-moons, just standard, but when helping someone with a problem, my new technique seems to create the right ambience.

'It's on the one hand more direct,' I muse to myself, 'since there are no lenses in the way. And yet it is at the same time less direct, since the student sinks into a fuzzy soft focus.' Maybe this new modus operandi gives me a much-needed and long overdue sense of gravitas?

I sigh. There are so many things to notice about teaching. I was once told that an art is any activity with more than seven variables.

'In which case,' I think, as I answer Annie's query with my new and benign myopia, 'teaching is an art seventy times over.'

Barry

St Philip Howard was blessed with a friendly yet hard-headed caretaking team, and their room became something of a refuge for me at the end of a long day. They were led by Barry, a grizzled old-timer who'd seen it all. His advice on my predicament was blunt.

'Easiest job in the world, being a bloody maths teacher,' he opined, sipping from a huge mug of tea. 'Especially now you've got this sodding Smiley maths to work with. No, Jonny, mate, I'd wake up in the morning and think, "If I can't bamboozle those little fuckers, I deserve all I've got coming to me." '

I took my own sip from an even bigger mug. Barry's hot-drink-making abilities were legendary; he made the humble tea-bag sing. I reflected on his idea of bamboozling students; it was not a way of working that my teaching course had emphasized. Maybe I should give it a go?

The next day, I wanted Leo for a detention at the close of play. I didn't think he'd come, and I said so in the staff room at lunch. Christina said that she had Leo last lesson, and that she would hold him for me. So at four o'clock I walked along to her room, and was able to feign surprise at seeing Leo. Leo knew he'd been outmaneuvered; he came with me like a lamb and did the full detention.

'Maybe I should do more of this,' I thought. 'Conspiring with fellow members of staff against students; is that the way forward?'

Always Read The Question

Richard, a statistics student of mine, hands in his answer to a line–of–best–fit exercise. The idea here is to take a scatter diagram of points showing two variables (a classic example would be to record shoe size and height for a class), and to try to add a straight line that approximates to the points as best you can.

Broadly speaking, we would expect people who have larger feet to be taller, but we would also expect the correlation to be approximate. We can add the line of best fit (by eye) like so, which helps us to roughly predict someone's height given their shoe size.

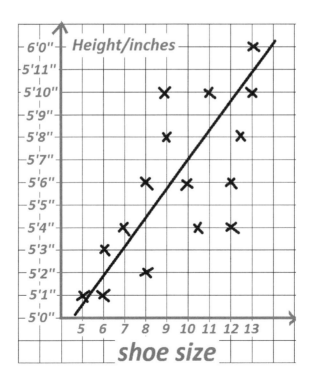

Could we not calculate the line of best fit from the data, rather than simply using our intuition? Indeed, 17-year-olds are called upon to do this, and Richard had succeeded. The task began:

The 1980 and 2000 catalogue prices, in pence, of five British postage stamps are as follows:

Is it me, or are we in danger of being whisked away into the world of mathematics question–speak? What's the chance that Richard is into stamps? I grimly wonder whether the writer of the question is or knows a philatelist. The problem goes on:

One stamp was valued at £5 in 1980 and at £62 in 2000. Comment.

The setter's idea was to encourage some reference to the line of best fit, but Richard gave this baffled but pithy answer:

What loser spends £62 on a stamp?

Learners have to negotiate more than mathematics when they attempt a maths examination. The rubric can be a trial, the language of the questions may be unfamiliar, and above all, the questions may embody a culture that is alien to our youngsters. Might that culture include philately?

Examiners sometimes try to move in the opposite direction, by attempting to appear 'totally chilled'. Inevitably young people rumble the authority figure aspiring to be trendy. Maybe they would rather have questions about £62 stamps than ones about buying an *Antarctic Gibbons* CD. No better than bringing in Stanley Gibbons, then.

94

Take this mechanics exam question. It concerns a piano and its owner's desire to shift it. Who should set about this task? Time to rent a cheerful chappie.

Arthur tries to move it by pulling with a force of 800 N…

Alf is clearly something of a cowboy in the piano–shifting world, because he quickly discovers he needs assistance.

Arthur is now joined by Barney and Chas…

Good move! But surely if Chas is involved, it won't long before…

Dave joins the other three and pulls with a force of (100i + 10j)…

What do students subliminally learn from this? Possibly that it's only men who can shift pianos, and only then if their names follow in alphabetical order, and only then if they wear cloth caps and whistle through gaps in their teeth.

I sigh. It's tempting to write a riposte from across the class divide.

Justin lies at one end of 12 ft. punt. He is holding a bottle of Bollinger in the water to cool. Suddenly the bottle's cork is expelled with a velocity of 10 m/s at an angle of 32 degrees. Miles is standing pole in hand at the other end of the punt, and he is 1.67m tall. The cork strikes him on the forehead while still rising. The cork returns directly towards the centre of the punt. Here it would strike Tristan on the chin, if only he had one…

I see irate examiners, shaking their heads at my facetiousness. I sigh again. The more I think about it, the harder the examiner's job becomes. Questions have to live in some context or other. But the set of mathematics question–writers is unlikely to be a representative sample from the population, and so their concerns won't be either. Bamboozling students from earthier backgrounds with unremittingly middle–class question scenarios is unfair. I've taught students who don't know the composition of a pack of cards. But then, it could be argued, here's their chance to learn.

Sigh number three. You can't please all of the people all of the time. When it comes to stereotyping, I'm as guilty as the next man–woman-person. Maybe I need to apologise to anyone out there called Arthur. Or Justin. And indeed, anyone who collects stamps?

You Can't Make Me

I see a girl looking really, really, fed up. Her name is Sarah, and she's gazing out of the window resentfully. Application of Number Level Two is clearly not her current place of choice. I decide to take a breezy approach.

'Sarah, you look awful: has your dog just died?' I ask lightly.

'Yes...' she says. The thought seems to cross her mind – *at least this is a game to be playing along with...*

'What was he called?' I enquire.

'Er... Rover.'

'How long have you had him?' I persist. Suddenly the game stops being fun.

'I hate maths. I really don't want to be here.'

'Have you tried the question?' I ask.

'I don't understand any of it.'

'Look, I'll help. You've drawn a rectangle, this one; what's its area?'

'I don't know and I don't care.'

'So why are you here?'

'I was told that the government insists that I am here.'

'And you resent that?'

'I resent that totally.'

'What else are you studying?'

'A levels in English, Art and Media, and IT Key Skills. I've got lots else to work on. I don't need maths.'

'But if you carpet your home? Won't you need to know about area?'

'I will ask someone, a friend, who does know about area.'

At this point, I say a number of things to myself.

The first is, *Jonny, you are a charlatan, a total fraud, a completely crap teacher. If you were halfway decent in the classroom, you'd surely be able to provide Sarah with a reasonably enjoyable maths experience. Hand in your resignation and start selling insurance, today!*

This is swiftly followed by, *Sarah, you ungrateful hussy, I've thought hard about this lesson, and the least you can do is give it a go! Do you realise how unemployable you will be without a Level 2 Maths qualification? So get real and knuckle down!*

This thought comes next: *This girl's being tortured. She has tried this subject for years and years and has never enjoyed a moment. She has developed a phobia over maths that makes her borderline special* needs. *I'm her torturer, and as the world has so painfully learnt, saying, "I'm simply following orders" is no defence.*

Now I catch the voice of our Vice–Principal; *Jonny, the college needs the money! If Sarah drops out we lose the funding not just for her maths course, but for all her key skills work, for all her tutorial work and for all her enrichment. Making maths optional will sink the college! Keep her in the room whatever!*

I hear myself again: *Sarah is now sixteen, she has freely decided to continue her education at a sixth form college, and she has chosen all her other subjects. Society sets an Age of Consent that she has passed, but for some reason the Mathematical Age of Consent is higher. She says this is both bizarre and unfair, and I cannot disagree with her.*

I come out of my reverie to see Sarah looking at me, concerned.

'Jonny, you look awful: has your dog just died?'

Mini–Theorems

We live in an age where there are huge banks of resources that a teacher can call upon. Many websites offer their mathematical wares for free. Long gone are the days when a teacher simply ploughed through the textbook without calling on any outside help. Sometimes producing your own material can even be frowned upon. 'You should be using stuff that more than one person has thought about,' said an advisor to me once.

Yet every teacher from time to time writes their own resources. You may have had an original idea that you're curious about, or you may want something you can't immediately lay your hands on. There's something exciting about trying out an idea of your own – can you make this work? I loved writing fresh tasks for my students, and the fact that my colleagues around the country and even further afield have found my creations useful too makes the kick even greater.

So I'm going to make the crazy assumption that you might be interested in what actually goes through the head of a maths teacher when they build a fresh task for their students. Say I want my students to consolidate their knowledge of fractions. Let's add that although this is consolidation, these are students still feeling their way into their fractional worlds.

I decide on these key skills that I want to reinforce:

1. ordering fractions, by size.
2. multiplying fractions together.
3. adding fractions together.

Now I could set:

Option One, a back–breaking set of exercises to practise the required skills,

or

Option Two, an extended slow–burn exercise, in part generated by the students themselves, that practises the required skills en passant and that works towards a 'mini–theorem'. I want to bring off a magic trick of sorts, and to stimulate discussion along the way.

Of course, Option Two picks itself. This route is more likely to engender a spirit of curiosity in the room, and curiosity is the vital force that makes learning fun. I want my students to explore, to become engrossed. The sweetest feeling for me as maths teacher is to look around the room, and see students so wrapped up in their work that I might as well not be there.

Option One would probably keep my more cautious students happy, but others would complain, 'I'm bored!', and lapse into chat.

So I start on writing the task.

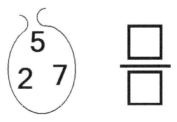

Every resource writer has their house style, and mine is to draw a bag with objects in (eventually I'll ask students to pick their own objects for the bag, so they've helped in writing the question. This small personal investment leads to caring more about the final outcome).

I ask how the objects could be used to produce another object (in this case a fraction).

Pick two numbers from the bag
and put them into the squares to make a fraction.

How many fractions could I produce? There are three ways to pick the top number, and three ways to pick the bottom number, so that's

3 × 3 = 9 fractions.

But allowing repeats produces $\frac{5}{5}$, $\frac{2}{2}$, and $\frac{7}{7}$, which would all be 1.
Now I'm planning to ask my students to put the fractions in order, so I'd prefer differently-sized fractions. So I change the wording:

Pick two numbers from the bag (no repeats!)
and put them into the squares to make a fraction.

So now I have 3 possibilities for the numerator, and once this has been chosen, 2 possibilities for the denominator, giving 6 fractions altogether. Placing six fractions in order is enough for this to be a meaningful task.

But hold on; if I pick 2, 4 and 8 in the bag; then $\dfrac{4}{2} = \dfrac{8}{4}$. So to get 6 differently-sized fractions, it helps to add this:

Extra rule: no pair of your numbers should have a common factor.

Notice now how the task is beginning to test extra ideas; the idea of a common factor is always worth revising.

How many different fractions can you make? Write them down.

Put the fractions you have into order.

It's fair to ask when contemplating a fraction, 'Does my denominator look big in this?' Large bottoms make for small fractions (unless the top is large too). What other rules do we have for comparing fractions? What if the tops are equal? Or the bottoms? Which are bigger than 1, and which are smaller? How do I compare $\dfrac{2}{5}$ with $\dfrac{5}{7}$? I'm really hoping profitable discussion will take place.

Our six fractions in order are $\dfrac{2}{7}, \dfrac{2}{5}, \dfrac{5}{7}, \dfrac{7}{5}, \dfrac{5}{2}, \dfrac{7}{2}$. The rotational symmetry about the central point is worth noting.

What do we get if we multiply all the fractions?

$$\frac{2}{7} \times \frac{2}{5} \times \frac{5}{7} \times \frac{7}{5} \times \frac{5}{2} \times \frac{7}{2}$$

103

The product is 1, whatever the numbers in the bag. This helps me; wandering round the room, I can look out for the value 1, and know that whatever numbers were chosen initially, the right maths probably ensued.

What do we get if we add all the fractions?

Adding fractions is harder than multiplying them; I need to bring in equivalent fractions. For our numbers,

$$\frac{2}{7} + \frac{2}{5} + \frac{5}{7} + \frac{7}{5} + \frac{5}{2} + \frac{7}{2} = \frac{20 + 28 + 50 + 98 + 175 + 245}{70} = \frac{616}{70} = \frac{44}{5}.$$

I pause. What would be really nice is for the six fractions to add to the same thing each time. Is there any way I could fix that?

$$\frac{a}{b} + \frac{a}{c} + \frac{b}{a} + \frac{b}{c} + \frac{c}{a} + \frac{c}{b} = \frac{a+b}{c} + \frac{b+c}{a} + \frac{c+a}{b}.$$

Hmm. If I put $a + b = c$, $b + c = a$, $c + a = b$, then I get 3 every time.

But these three equations solve to give $a = b = c = 0$, which isn't much use.

Hang on! If I say instead $a + b = -c$, $b + c = -a$, $c + a = -b$, then I get -3 every time, and the equations all reduce to $a + b + c = 0$.

So we have a way of fixing this magic trick; we insist

the three numbers chosen at the start add to zero.

I can now type up the finished task.

The Fractions-from-a-Bag Problem

Pick three different non-zero whole numbers that add to 0,
and put them into a bag.

Extra rule: no pair of your numbers should have a common factor.

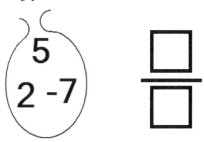

Now pick two numbers from the bag (no repeats!)
and put them into the squares to make a fraction.

How many different fractions can you make? Write them down.

Put the fractions you have into order.

What do we get if we multiply all the fractions?

What do we get if we add all the fractions?

Compare notes on this with your colleagues.

Can you prove this will always work?

There's the magic trick for the last part - we get -3 every time! Why?
We can make 6 different fractions,

$$\frac{a}{b}, \frac{c}{b}, \frac{a}{c}, \frac{b}{c}, \frac{a}{b}, \text{ and } \frac{c}{a}.$$

Adding them gives

$$\frac{a+c}{b} + \frac{a+b}{c} + \frac{b+c}{a}$$

$$= \frac{-b}{b} + \frac{-c}{c} + \frac{-a}{a}$$

$$= -3.$$

The task feels neat. It counts as differentiated – everyone will be able to pick some numbers to get started, but there are layers of difficulty, and not everyone may get as far as proving the final challenge.

I sit back, satisfied. Here's a pleasing twist – the key words

that add to 0,

which conclude the first line of the task, were, in fact, the last part of the problem to be written.

Tony

My emotional helter-skelter in Tower Hamlets had reached month three. I was having an especial battle with the second-set group of fifteen-year-olds, a bunch of street-wise wise-crackers who varied, let's say, in their commitment to achieving GCSE maths in a few months' time.

The stand-out (loudest) student was a lad called Tony Tomlinson, who was extraordinarily uninhibited and answered to no one, not even to Margaret. His dad was a plumber, and had the school-leaving age been 14, Tony would have been working for him by now. School for the Tomlinson family had thus become a legal obligation, an annoying pain, in fact, which is why Tony approached the institution as a kind of open prison. He had six months of his sentence left, and if a teacher-screw got in the way, too bad.

'Here we go, here we go, here we go,' he sang mid-lesson, as he picked up one of my metre rules, and jammed it down his left inside trouser leg. The class was then treated to a series of goosesteps around the room, accompanied by chants, thankfully non-Nazi ones. There were girls in the room who wanted to get on, and they sat, resigned and scornful, with arms folded. There's often talk in schools about students who 'steal the education of others'. Tony did not so much steal his colleagues' education as produce a gun and hold them up for it, before setting it on fire and dancing over its ashes.

Student misbehaviour makes me pause. It's wrong to always blame the students for playing up; sometimes your lesson is so misconceived they won't be able to take part sensibly with the best will in the world. It's easy when up against it to teach defensively, by which I mean you set something that's bulletproof in an overly routine way, something simple to administer but where educational considerations have come a long way down the list of priorities. I found myself thinking at anxious moments at the start of my career, 'They're only a worksheet away'. The weak teacher always thinks of their own survival above everything else. The students can rightly ask here for more interesting work to be set.

Then there are those students who feel they just aren't cut out for school, who sense that it's a system at which they are preordained to fail, and where they feel they can only preserve their self-esteem by impressing their similarly-placed peers through cool horseplay. Maybe these youngsters would be better off as apprentices, pulling a wage (as long as we make it easy for them to change their mind later and pick up qualifications then if they want to).

But none of this applied to Tony, whose boring badinage masked genuine mathematical ability. My lessons were carefully planned, and with a reasonably willing participation from my pupils, they would've been adjudged worthwhile if not scintillating. Tony didn't have 'anger issues' or epilepsy or a tricky family background; he was just a bloke who liked being blokey.

I often wonder now what happened to Tony. Maybe he'd turned out to be a crap plumber, and his father had got shot of him at the earliest opportunity. Maybe Tony found himself sitting in front of daytime TV, watching the game show repeats and unable to answer a single question. Maybe he'd wandered down the Jobcentre out of boredom one day, and asked about a job, leaning back in his chair (old habits die hard).

'We do have something that might suit you, Mr Tomlinson, but it does require GCSE Maths. Have you passed that?'

Just remember, Tony, I was there, offering you such a thing, and you declined. Yes, you did, Tony, you were bright enough it get it, but you opted instead for those metre rule goose-steps. What's that? If I'd been a better teacher, I would have stopped you? If you'd been a better student, I wouldn't have needed to.

When I watch inner city riots on the TV, enacted by disaffected youth after some police mistake, I look out for a wild lad with a ruler down his trousers running uncomfortably away from the baton charges. What a shame there wasn't a GCSE in that, Tony; you would have walked (still uncomfortably) an A*. And when a sociologist comes on next, bleating about 'You know, the oppressed underclass,' I think, *I can't feel sorry for you, Tony. You know what? More fool you.*

Didn't I Teach You Something Once?

It's the first day of the holidays, and I celebrate by watching the first few hours of the first Ashes test. Glenn McGrath takes his 500th test wicket, and holds the ball aloft.

'He can remember every one of those wickets,' says Ritchie Benaud. 'Test him on the 364th, and he'll tell you who it was.'

I wonder, how do I feel about students I once taught? Some of my colleagues recall every face that has passed through their classroom, with every grade they achieved in every exam etched onto their memory. Others concentrate solely on the young people before them, passing ex–students in the street without a glance and consigning old markbooks to the bin as last year's harvest.

'Which camp am I in?' I reflect. On the one hand, I can't help but remember students I've spent a lot of class-time with, and of whom I've become remarkably fond (in a teacherly way) by the end of it all. It'd be simply bizarre to have no interest in what happens to them next.

But another part of me says, let your past students go. I always feel as I throw out old coursework that I'm liberating the young people who produced it. The reason we knew each other was to learn maths together: that reason has run its course, so let's say goodbye, in a spirit of thankfulness for the things that went well, and forgiveness for the things that didn't.

The issue is live for me now, as Pete and Diana, two of my ex–students, visited the College yesterday to talk to our Further Mathematicians. Each took a maths degree at our local university, and both are now midway through their PhDs. They kindly agreed to come back to give our students an insight into being a full-time research mathematician. How must it feel to be pushing back the boundaries of the subject?

'You take this elliptic curve...' says Pete, as the overhead projector whirrs in front of a rapt audience, and I'm awestruck at how technically assured they both now are. Part of my reaction is selfish, but also human; I can't help wondering how much credit I should take for the brilliance they've now attained. 'Not much,' I decide in the end, 'but I can't have done too much damage either.' The talks both go well, as Pete and Diana provide excellent role–models for those of our students thinking of doing something mathematical at university. The questions afterwards are disarming:

'What's it like doing a PhD – is it competitive?'

'How did you pick your question to research in the first place?'

'Don't you ever worry that you'll put three years in on your question and not get an answer?'

Pete and Diana both laugh, nervously. On the long and lonely road that is a PhD, such thoughts must come to haunt you in the middle of the night.

It's mid–morning, and the guests, after enjoying their coffee and biscuits, have left. I belatedly sign Diana in for a security badge before our walk around College. 'What 's your car number–plate?' I ask.

Diana, who's just been writing thirteen–digit primes on the board from memory, has a think. 'Blimey, that's a tough one...'

111

Let's Quote Maths

It's a common scene in a classroom; a student throws something, another throws it back. I've been known to quote Gandhi's famous truism to the second of the pair, 'An eye for an eye will turn the whole world blind.' I ran into unexpected trouble over this with Terry once. 'Aw, quotes are for losers,' he said disgustedly (I naturally noted this down for use on a future occasion).

Here's a cheery game to fill an idle moment; take a popular quotation, and mathematise it as best you can. For example, 'If mathematics did not exist, it would be necessary to invent it.' It's remarkable how easily most quotations translate across. I'm fond of this one: 'To be or not to be, that is the Law of the Excluded Middle' (mathematicians allow a statement to be true or false but nothing in between). Or you might look at binary notation, where every number can be expressed using just the digits 0 and 1, and say, 'Never has so much been owed by so many numbers to so few.' Of course, this levity relies on a little general knowledge on the part of your students; if they equate Churchill with a nodding dog, then you're likely to appear a touch eccentric.

Sometimes these mongrel efforts can provide helpful insight, maybe even more so than the original. Another Gandhi quotation I like, for its toe-curling qualities, is this; 'Everyone in the world would be a Christian if only it wasn't for the Christians.' This naturally mathematises to, 'Everyone in the world would be a mathematician if only it wasn't for the mathematicians,' which has a horribly true ring to it. Maybe we maths teachers are justified in trying to spread the gospel of mathematics, but the gospel we attempt to spread is too often a parody of the real thing.

Another couple suggest themselves; how about doctoring the clear tones of John F. Kennedy? 'Ask not what mathematics can do for you, ask what you can do for mathematics!' That seems to set the bar impossibly high, but if you can jump over that, then as Kipling (almost) once said, 'And then – which is more – you'll be a mathematician, my son!'

Theo's Law

Theo is someone I respect; he's someone high up in maths education, and he's someone who once taught in a maths classroom. With some remorse, he regards that as a time when he was a doer, before becoming someone who either thinks about doing, or who watches other people doing. Down the years he's developed a law which runs as follows:

Your credibility as a mathematics educator C is inversely proportional to the time t that's passed since you last earned your living by teaching in a classroom.

In other words,

$$C = \frac{k}{t}$$

for some constant k.

There's a humility built into Theo's Law. Every day that passes, according to Theo, means that he has less credibility over maths education matters.

I've tested Theo's Law in the field, and I've found that it needs tweaking. In fact, I would say more precisely that

$$C = \frac{k\,s}{t}$$

where s = the strength with which you believe Theo's Law (s can vary over time).

Using this revision, I estimate that Theo's credibility as a maths educator has been growing steadily for a while.

114

BISS

At the start of my second term in Tower Hamlets, I was becoming frayed enough for my first BISS lesson.

Maybe every teacher that makes it has this. Some have it sooner than others; maybe quick developers make their very first lesson BISSful. There are those who agonise about their right to impose anything upon their charges, and who wonder whether their feelings about making their classroom democratic should be explored openly with each class. It's these teachers who are likely to delay their entry into BISSfulness. Others, who trust what they find themselves wanting for their students without even thinking about it, swiftly enter BISSitude.

So a teacher sets up a framework in the classroom, to be followed by not only the students but also the teacher themself, a framework that's reasonable and which has been negotiated, with sanctions that have been agreed. What can go wrong? Yet every teacher on a bad day in their probationary year finds themselves with anger rising in their gullet as mayhem surrounds them, and a perfectly reasonable request they have made to an idle child receives the reply, 'Why?'

Something snaps, and the BISS moment arrives.

'Because I said so!'

I fought off my entry into BISShood for months, but eventually I succumbed. Paul was being especially difficult, and I decided to move him.

'Paul, could you please pick up your things, and come and sit over here!'

Paul stuck out his jaw, and with a decent audience to spur him on said, 'Why?' as he turned his back.

Completely without premeditation, the four words came out.

'Because I said so!' Exasperation tumbled out into the room.

But this was the East End.

'Ha, ha, ha!' Half the room was now in stitches. Paul turned back to me appreciatively.

'Oh, yes, sir, with the getting-hard skills!'

Apparently no progress then. But there had, in fact, been a change in me.

I don't actually think the reason, 'Because I said so!' is a particularly good one. I do believe in aiming for a classroom that's a democracy of sorts. But a teacher must lead; if they're not prepared to take that role on, they're in the wrong job. When student delaying tactics reach an unacceptable level, I would say BISS has a place. And if I need a variation, JUDI is on hand; 'Just do it!'

It Doesn't Matter!

It's Friday lunchtime, and my classroom is hosting a CAROM session (Creative Activities Resulting in Offbeat Mathematics). We're not a large group, five or six, but each week we meet to discuss beautiful bits of mathematics that the syllabus in its wisdom decrees are less essential than The Useful Stuff like partial fractions, vectors and the Sine Rule (although I realise these are beautiful too in their own way).

I look on amazed. My fellow CAROMites are leaning back in their seats, howling with laughter.

'So it doesn't matter!' they're screaming. 'Brilliant! It doesn't matter!'

So how had I provoked my group into this ribaldry?

'Today's topic is infinity…' I'd begun, innocently enough.

Ten minutes later: 'Ah! So the infinity describing the rationals and the infinity describing the natural numbers must be the same,' says Beth.

Five minutes on: 'Ah! So the infinity represented by the real numbers must be a bigger infinity than this,' exclaims Stephen.

Breathlessly I asked, 'Might there not be an infinity between these two infinities? Kurt Godel showed in 1940 that it was impossible to prove that such an infinity exists…'

My voice became reverential: 'Then in 1963, Paul Cohen showed that it was impossible to prove that such an infinity does not exist!

Mathematics works perfectly well either way! So you can't decide if this middle infinity exists or not – it doesn't matter!'

Somehow the idea that the crowning achievement of your life should be the phrase, 'It doesn't matter!' had struck my disrespectful protégés as completely hilarious.

'What a good day's work that was! Ha, ha, ha!' said Anandi.

Our session about the Riemann Hypothesis had gone the same way. This is arguably the most fundamental unsolved problem in mathematics. It is hard to explain simply, but it says in effect that all the non-trivial zeros taken by a particular function all lie on a particular line in the complex plane. The first few billion have been checked, and they all behave so far, but the next one might not…

'Someone once said,' I quoted, '*If the Riemann Hypothesis were to be proved false, our world would collapse. So much has been built upon assuming that it is true.*'

Nicky starts to improvise. 'So he comes downstairs, and his wife says…'

'Oh, love, there was something on the radio about a zero being found off some line or other…' says Stephanie. 'Supper's ready!'

'Are you feeling alright, love?' says William.

My students' view was that on the day that someone proved or disproved the Riemann Hypothesis, most people would have breakfast

118

as usual, go to work relatively calmly on buses and tubes, and sleep soundly after a quiet evening in.

I was reminded of the story about the man who built his house upon sand, and the man who built his house upon a rock. Maybe there's no completely certain rock on which to build in mathematics, but some pieces of ground are likely to be safer than others. If you devote your life to theorems that are contingent on other, as yet unproved, theorems, you may get what's coming to you.

I look around me. The laughter my students are enjoying is not malicious (well, not <u>really</u> malicious). It's just that if you choose to work on a topic that only a handful of people in the world care about or understand, that impinges so slightly on the world of 'ordinary' people, how can you expect sympathy when things go wrong?

'I told you he should've got out more…'

The Evolution of Words

Sometimes there's a language gap in my classroom. Take the other day; my lesson grinds to a halt as Jacob theatrically (and pathetically) hides Matt's phone.

'Jacob, you're a real wag,' I say, to complete silence.

'Why are you calling Jacob a wife and girlfriend?' asks Gwyn.

'I'll try again - Jacob, you are a real card,' I say.

The blank looks are universal once more.

'What's the matter with the youth of today,' I ask, peevishly. 'Can't you understand plain English?'

This interaction took me back to life in Tower Hamlets, where language was frequently morphed in wonderful ways. The blank looks on these occasions were all mine. Two linguistic transformations stay with me; nothing was ever stolen, but taxed, and I never taught anyone anything, I always learnt it to them. Conversations would go like this;

Me: Lee, where's your pen?

Lee: Stuart taxed it.

Me: Look, borrow this - what are you working on?

Lee: Aw, it's area - can you learn me this, sir?

Any right-wingers reading this (welcome to the book) will be nodding with approval at the notion that the verb 'tax' equates with 'steal'. And 'Can you learn me this?' – I prefer that version. Teaching upside down…

Fermat's Last Theorem

The last lesson of any term is tricky. Students sense the impending holidays, so some teachers feel any attempt to teach to the final moment is doomed. My way out (for Christmas Year 1 at least) is to show Simon Singh's famous documentary on Andrew Wiles' solution of Fermat's Last Theorem. This 50 minutes represents, I humbly claim, the best mathematics ever filmed. I must have watched this thirty times now – as a devout believer learns their sacred text by heart, so I can remember every word and every camera angle, and the programme still reduces me to tears every time. The video opens with Andrew (it feels wrong to call him 'Wiles' here) on the edge of tears himself ('Bless!' said Craig), as he tries to convey what finding his proof meant to him. My students may have cried about maths themselves, but never for heart-warming reasons, and to meet this charming if awkward man who'd been so moved by mathematics is startling for them.

'Is this going to be funny?' Mark asks me.

Two minutes in, and we get a full view of Andrew's desk, which is literally a foot deep in papers, journals, doodling and doubtless the odd biscuit.

'I thought you said this wasn't going to be funny,' Mark says (the desire to offer a commentary on any piece of TV is irresistible for any class).

'So here was this problem that I, a ten–year–old, could understand', says Andrew ('a pretty bright ten–year–old', sniffed Darren). We learn how Andrew decided to work alone on this problem for seven years, night and day, without telling any colleague what he was doing.

122

'Don't mathematicians share their stuff?' asks Kay in some annoyance, and it seems that some of the other mathematics professors at Princeton, a truly stellar list of names, agree with her.

'I told my wife that I was working on Fermat…'

'He's married! No! Really?'

The programme reaches its climax as Andrew explains his final step.

'Do you understand this stuff, Jonny?' asks Ronnie innocently, and I shift a little uneasily in my seat. 'Oh yes, no problem.'

Then the story takes a twist – there's a mistake in Andrew's proof. Here's something all my young learners can appreciate; you hand in your work, it's marked, and you've got something wrong. Andrew's mistake is one that maybe only three people in the world could have spotted, but it is one, none the less. So the programme has a second climax, as Andrew, after intense pain, resolves his error.

Afterwards I show my students the first page of the proof. The first line is: *Let p be an odd prime*. I watch my students relax: hey, this proving Fermat's Last Theorem stuff is easy. The second line is: *Let Σ be a finite set of primes including p and let Q_Σ be the maximal extension of Q unramified about this set.* I screw up my eyes: 'extension' maybe I could begin to guess at, but 'maximal extension'? 'Unramified'? I have not the remotest idea what these things mean. There are another 20 lines to this page, that appear to grow in difficulty as they go on, and a further 100 pages after that.

'I've had the rare privilege,' Andrew says in the film, 'of being able to pursue my childhood dream in my adult life.' I look around my class as they troop out – what are your childhood dreams, and will they be fulfilled?

'And what were my dreams at your age?' I wonder. They were, like Andrew's, of proving things. Maybe it's not too late…

Take a Seat

It's our first lesson in January, and I'm unpopular. I've unveiled a seating plan, and my Statistics group are grumbling. All those friendship groups (that are, frankly, a lot more fun than anything I have to say) have now been thrown into turmoil; the dice have been rolled, and some find themselves working with near–strangers.

It's also the time of year when we ask for student feedback. I give out the mini–questionnaires, and groaning again, most of my charges immediately tick Box 2 (agree) for everything. Comments are invited, but there's only one, from Phil:

Why do we have a seating plan? This is stupid. It seems a childish thing to do, especially at sixth form.

I am surprised at the force of this. Phil is a superb student, a certainty for an A Grade in Maths, who plans to become an engineer and he'll doubtless make an excellent one. He's mature, hardworking, and heavily involved with our Student Council. Our relationship has until today been without friction of any kind, if you leave out the static and kinetic varieties. He's clearly been angered by my new arrangement. One of the questionnaire statements is

So far the course has been taught in a way that suits me,

and he's ticked

Strongly Disagree.

I've placed him on a table with Sam, who's clearly unhappy too. The other tables seem calmer. Of course, I may not have the whole story. Is there some history between Sam and Phil? If my seating plan is too rigid to be tweaked, then that's a problem.

I don't like upsetting any students, let alone students that are hard to upset. As I sit in front of my computer this evening, I feel I owe it to Phil to try to explain myself. Was my re–seat just a piece of friendship–bashing control–freakery, or is there method in my madness? After all, it's rare for an A Level classroom to be organised in this way. The vast majority of the time with sixth-formers, friends enjoy each other's company quietly, and harness that friendship to learn profitably together. Do Sam and Phil have a point?

What happens in the maths classroom will always be a social experience, and part of the teacher's task is to make it a fulfilling one. It's hopeless to imagine that students will somehow take off their friendships like so many coats and hang them at the door on their way in. Friendship is the bee's knees, for all of us. Indeed, do I feel a little jealousy of the friendships that Phil has? At my age now, close friendships seem rarer and more precious to me than they were when I was Phil's age.

But the cultivation of friendship is not the main reason we've come together. We're in a maths classroom first and foremost to learn maths. If that's forgotten, any 'friendship' resulting will be spurious. If friendship ever impedes the learning, then a change is needed.

Let me ask a few questions; if given a free choice on where to sit,

Do popular students tend to sit together?

126

Do the boys tend to sit together?
Do the loud students tend to sit together?
Do the bright students tend to sit together?
Do year–groups tend to sit together?
Are these arrangements desirable when it comes to learning maths?

Phil is a Year 13 student, and Sam is Year 12. In this group (unusually) there are eight Year 12 students and seven Year 13 students. The Year 12 students have always sat together, as have the Year 13. Phil tends to sit in a group of four close Year 13 friends. Prior to my intervention, I would look out over the class and sense an unhealthy atmosphere – is this one class I am teaching, or two?

Michael Marland says this in *The Craft of the Classroom*:

Often teachers allow virtually impenetrable small groups to bring their sealing–off relationships into the classroom. Thus the teacher is unable to develop a truly individual approach to Joan, as she is always part of the Siamese twin, 'Joan and Lorraine'.

Is Phil usually part of a Siamese quadruplet in my class?

Some recent research compared the educational outcomes on a task accomplished by;
1. groups chosen along friendship lines
2. groups where each contained a stranger.
The friendship groups had more fun, but the groups containing a stranger made much more progress with the task.

There's much current discussion in the media over the words 'multi–culturalism' and 'integration.' Bringing that down to the micro level of my classroom, for me, integration is vital. A baker begins by surveying the yeast, the flour, and the water. To create bread, the ingredients need to be merged and kneaded; unlikes need to meet to become one and thus productive. I prefer to look out on a class that's mixed up (let's face it, I am, so the class might as well be). If I see a class containing ghettos and cliques, where every table is either a Girls Aloud or a Boyzone, then I know the learning suffers. Somehow too in such a situation, I feel excluded; can I play too?

So what will I do when I see Phil next, beyond thanking him for his honesty? Maybe I will suggest that the good thing about a re–seat is that unexpected joys can result. I often introduce such a plan by saying, while adding a pinch of corn to my voice; 'Please regard this as a chance for new and beautiful relationships to form between you.'

My words are not without irony, but I'm trying to convey a truth too. A strong student may discover a talent for teaching when placed next to a weaker student, a talent that would otherwise have remained dormant. A weaker student may have been in awe of a brighter colleague, only to find that there's nothing scary when they share a table. One student may have unconsciously written off another as a person; when placed together, he discovers he was wrong to do so. It could be that in two lessons' time, Phil and Sam will be getting on like blood brothers. In fact, I can already hear them complaining about my NEXT resit.

If It's Not Broken, Break It

Halfway through my first year, and the trench warfare at Tower Hamlets rumbled on. Occasionally we would hit a part of the syllabus where students would naturally fly. The Mathematical Model-Making Module, otherwise known as M^4, was a huge success, but I found harnessing good energy here as tough as dampening down malignant energy elsewhere.

I thought back to my teaching practice. My supervisor had eyed me sagely as I analysed the lesson he'd just witnessed, which had been rocky (I'll confess, I've never been a natural disciplinarian). He sat back in his chair.

'I had trouble with classes when I started out, Jonny. All over the place. The stress began to get to me. Then one day, I said, "I'm going to break this one class." Just one. I threw the book at them. It took me a term, but I then had that one class exactly where I wanted them. And then I went through all my other classes, just like that.'

He clicked his fingers three times.

'Something comes into your voice when you've broken a class. The kids can hear it. And after that, you never have to work hard at discipline ever again.'

As I drove into that East End school each morning, those words bounced around my head. Was this what I had to do?

I can say now, I don't believe in breaking classes, and I'm not sure I ever did. You hear about managers trying to 'break' a rebellious employee; let's call that bullying. I don't want to teach students I've remorselessly punished into grudging silence, I want students whose drives are channelled creatively in an atmosphere of mutual respect.

But back in those Tower Hamlet days, I looked up in awe to those teachers whose cutting voices and piercing eyes were enough to command instant quiet with the toughest of classes. They seemed to combine hypnosis with a touch of threat.

By the end of my career, discipline had become a game in my class. I realised a drift in focus, a piece of chat, a digression, was a pointer to the fact that a small break was needed. So the secret was to try to respond to a bit of poor behaviour with humour, welcoming it as a chance to have a brief pause.

'Joe, what are you talking about?'

'We're discussing whether or not I'm psychic.'

'What am I going to say next?'

'You're going to give me a warning.'

'Correct.'

I've stepped over into boring Joe, or maybe the concentration I've been demanding from him is too much. So if I can manufacture a tiny smile for him, that may be all the break he needs.

We're All Special Needs

My class is thinking about averages. I trot out my standard line (every teacher has them) without thinking. 'You know, folks, almost everybody has more than the average number of legs.'

The idea I'm trying to get across is that the mean number of legs out there is, say, 1.99, so given that the vast majority of people have 2, my statement makes sense. (If by 'average' you read 'mode' or 'median', then it doesn't.)

I'm immediately struck dumb, as I remember that Roddy, a student in the group, was in a nasty car crash a few years ago which means he does in fact have a prosthetic leg. Fortunately, he's at ease with his disability.

'That doesn't work, Jonny,' he says with a smile. 'I've got five legs at home.'

There's been a welcome transformation in provision for those with disabilities in my time at Paston. Our classrooms have become vastly more accessible, and sensitivities over people's needs have multiplied (at least if I'm not stressed off my face and forget). Yet with increased awareness come more diagnoses. Invigilating seventeen students the other day, I found that seven qualify for different amounts of extra time for a range of reasons including dyslexia, poor handwriting and nervousness. When it came to exams last year one student offered his special need as 'an inability to work in silence'.

Sometimes 'normal' students are bewildered by this.

'Jonny, I'm just not very good at maths. Can't I have an extra fifteen minutes for that?'

Do they have a point? Without sounding too precious, are we not all special needs? I believe the L'Arche Communities for those with learning difficulties once had this in their charter:

We are all disabled in some way. One person's disability may be blindness, while another's may be selfishness.

We could include maths–phobia here too. Future generations may not look too kindly on the way we force so many suffering students to study mathematics when they are old enough to choose for themselves.

For a teacher, meeting the needs of those with disabilities is not always a straightforward issue. I vividly recall the start of one year, when I was told I was to be teaching a profoundly deaf student called Lorna. At the end of our first lesson, she had a chat.

'I've got a request, Jonny,' she asked with a smile. 'I can't lip–read properly with beards. I wonder, please, could you shave yours off?'

Hmm. Emotions immediately rushed in. One thought was,

'Of course, why not? I've spent most of my life without a beard, Lorna, and if it's a help to you, I'll remove it.'

But then, would acceding to such a personal request from a student, even for such an excellent reason, be entirely healthy? I'd shaved off my beard off at someone else's request only once before, when I joined a band doing Elvis covers; our leader pointed out to me that the great

132

man was decidedly clean–shaven. But was this new request a step too far? Surely Lorna would have to deal with beards in 'real life'? I remembered the story of Samson, whose power had drained away as he'd been shorn, and I felt something similar might happen in my classroom. And what would Lorna's second request be?

In the event, there was a coincidental re–jigging of the sets, and Lorna was whisked away into another group. So the immediate dilemma disappeared, but it was hardly dealt with. So here's a question for every excessively-bearded maths teacher out there; what would you have done?

Can Girls Do Maths?

I'm helping a group in one corner of my classroom when in another I hear Andrew muttering contemptuously, 'Bloody Muslims!' I'm unaware of teaching any Muslims in this class. He's a fundamentally decent lad who doesn't think too hard before speaking. I haul him out of the room, where he leans against the wall a tad sheepishly.

'Andrew, how much do you know about Islamic culture? Do you realise how the Arab world kept maths alive in the time between the Greeks and the Renaissance?' He looks at me uncomprehendingly.

'How many symmetry groups can you find on the walls of the Alhambra?' Unsurprisingly, again this means nothing to Andrew. Am I overdoing it? Risking the college harassment policy, I press on.

'Andrew, do you call your Islamic friends, "Bloody muslims"?' By now Andrew's head has well and truly dropped. He's got the message. Subdued, he returns to his group.

The population in Norfolk is monochrome - less than 1% of the county comes from an ethnic minority. This means that through no fault of their own, Norfolk students often find other cultures a challenge to their unchosen but insular world–view.

Later that day I get home and settle down to *The Independent* with a cup of tea. My eye is caught by an article headed, *The Price of Daring to Teach Girls.* It tells the story of Mr Usman, who along with his wife set up a secret school for girls in Afghanistan. The paper describes his fate simply: 'the Taliban beat him to death for teaching the girls algebra.'

Some people say that religion is a malignant virus, and that a world without it would be a better one. I would say that bad religion is indeed a grave problem, but that good religion is an incalculable blessing. Speak to a true Muslim, and one cannot fail to be drawn to the faith. Purity, truth and justice are the obvious fruits of a life spent worshipping Allah. But just as there are some Christians who hold to violence despite the peaceful intent of their founder, so too there are followers of the Prophet who place peace to one side.

Killing mathematics teachers for teaching girls? I feel like shouting, 'If you're in the Taliban, could you please doubt yourself sometimes? Try saying to yourself, "I might be wrong!" Please!'

It's rare for me to sense anger as strong as this. A powerful solidarity with Mr Usman well up within me, that he should lose his life pursuing our shared vocation. The contrast with my own life as a maths teacher is painful. For me, teaching algebra can feel like flogging a dead horse, but in Afghanistan it seems, teaching algebra to girls can mean being flogged until you might as well be a dead horse.

As Andrew could tell you after our conversation that morning, when it comes to encouraging an awareness of the riches of Islam, mathematics teachers the world over are well placed to help. Algebra is itself a word gifted to the world by Islam. I would say to the Taliban, 'Do you wish the mathematics teachers of the world to join in the fight against Islamophobia? Because if you do, you're making our job difficult. In fact, obscenely difficult.'

Mathematical Hypnotherapy

Martha's a friend of mine, a vivacious 23–year–old who has just completed a maths degree at Edinburgh University. Proudly clutching her First Class Honours, she's starting out as a statistician with a top London firm – the world lies at her feet. Yet two years ago all this apparently inevitable success was thrown into doubt when she awoke one morning to find she'd completely lost the use of her muscles. She lay prone until discovered by a housemate. An ordinary evening the night before led to this vast disability a few hours later.

Blood was taken, tests were run, doctors were mystified. Nothing physically adrift was found – Martha's body seemed to be in perfect shape, but was somehow sulking. Then the white–coated experts tried a remarkable experiment – they hypnotised Martha, and asked her to climb some stairs. Simple as it sounds, this task was on a par with scaling Everest without oxygen for Disabled Martha. But under this benign hypnosis, her muscles leapt into action, and she made it up and down the steps without a murmur. The boffins had thoughtfully recorded this ghostly activity, and were able to play the film back to Martha once she came round, to her total amazement. The endeavour revealed her ailment to be incontrovertibly all–in–the–mind.

There's no compelling evidence that this exercise was vital to her eventual recovery, but the story is thought-provoking. Hypnosis (and I don't mean purely making people think they are drunken elephants during a theatrical freak show) can be widely construed - any psychological trick that gets us to do someone's bidding without our fully realising why could to my mind count as hypnosis.

A doctor knows that to ask a boy, 'Can I look into your ears?' is inviting trouble. He asks instead, 'Which ear should I look in first, your left or your right?' Introducing this tiny choice leads to a happy child. Hypnosis?

How about the classroom? I would say the really successful disciplinarians amongst teachers all have a touch of the hypnotist. How, for example, do teachers ask for silence? I've tried various systems down the years for this, including ringing a bell. This met with a snort from Henrietta – 'I'm not a cow, you know!' – only for the rest of the group to chorus, 'Oh yes you are…'

I think 'Stop talking, please,' has its limitations. 'Give me your eyes and ears, thank you,' replaces a negative (stop) with a positive (do this) and replaces a request (please) with a self–fulfilling prophecy (thank you). Each of my students that hears this mantra will unconsciously identify with all of their previous colleagues who've quietened at my bidding, and I slowly develop 'a spell'.

Sometimes students can cast a spell over themselves, even curse themselves.

'I can't do fractions,' they say. I always attempt to break this hex.

'Try saying instead, "I can't do fractions at the moment." '

I would say our parents 'hypnotise' us as babies. To mature into adults is to learn to spot these familial techniques (that may be completely subconscious) and to free ourselves from them. There are often damaging family myths that tell us we cannot do things that, in fact, we can. And what for maths teachers is the most damaging family myth of all?

'Oh, he's never been able to do maths.'

So maybe part of my job is to gently hypnotise students whose mathematical muscles are really fine, but who are trapped into a negative view of themselves that leaves them arithmetically prone in maths classrooms. Hopefully safe in my hands, I can then ask them to walk up and down mathematical stairs, only to surprise them later when I show them what they've achieved. Maybe then they can go home and challenge family preconceptions. I wonder if every mathematics teacher can, even should, quietly be a hypnotherapist.

My Struggle

There's a famous rule governing social media conversations that goes under the name of Godwin's law; it says that as such a conversation increases in length, the probability of some kind of inflammatory comparison with the Nazis or Hitler approaches 1 (a probability of 1 represents, of course, certainty). A similar thing applies to the chance that a teacher will be likened at some stage in their career to Hitler or the Nazis. It took me twenty-one years, but I got there in the end.

The setting is a Further Maths group that's unusual in that four students have effectively been allowed to resit with a view to improving their grade. This seems like a soft decision by management to me; we get no funding for them, and as I mark their work at two in the morning, I wonder, 'Why am I doing this?' These students also carry into the lesson a blasé been-there-done-it attitude that's deeply unhelpful for all the regular bods doing the course for the first time. In addition, three of the returners play for the local rugby team, and they seem to view my lessons as psychological scrummaging practice. I've compared notes with David, my Head of Department, and we agree we have a problem. 'This is a Further Maths group,' David said. 'For crying out loud, this should be the most attentive bunch I see all week.'

Confrontation has become inevitable. Don annoys me once too often, and I ask him to move to the front of the class. 'Why?' he asks, jutting out his ample jaw.

'Just do it, Don,' I say, even more annoyed. Don gets up and moves to the seat I've given him.

'Ha! Just do it!' he says. 'That's the kind of logic Hitler used.'

Of course, it's a thick thing to say, and maybe a laugh from me is the best riposte, but it also needles. *Me? You are comparing me to Hitler?* Alongside my annoyance now sits a feeling of injustice.

'Don, I agree I'm like Hitler in some ways,' I perhaps foolishly continue. 'I don't eat meat. I don't drink alcohol. But I've never invaded Poland. I've not even visited Poland. And I think you'll find Hitler did worse things than ask someone to swap seats.'

'But Hitler was a dictator, Jonny.' Don the prop forward is locking heads with me yet again.

'You're right again, Don, this is not a democracy. You can't change your teacher by having a vote. But even so, I'd like to be a teacher that listens. In return, you need to listen to me. What am I saying? That the louder members of this group need to sober up, be more considerate, and concentrate.'

I scan the room. The first-timers are nodding. The second-timers look sheepish.

'Do this, and I'll become less like Hitler,' I say. 'But I'm still reserving the right to write a book that sells a copy or two, okay?'

But It Looks So Simple

I've yet to meet a mathematics teacher who isn't thankful for Goldbach's Conjecture. If asked for an example of how the most straightforward of questions can refuse to yield to the best efforts of the top mathematicians, this is the perfect riposte.

So what does Goldbach's Conjecture actually say?

Every even number greater than 2 can be written as the sum of two primes.

$$\text{So } 4 = 2+2, 6 = 3+3, 8 = 5 + 3, 10 = 3 + 7\dots$$

A prime number, you'll remember, is one that has only two divisors, itself and 1. The first few primes go

$$2, 3, 5, 7, 11, 13, 17, 19, 23, 29,\dots$$

The conjecture has been tested for the first few billion even numbers, and it has always checked out. To be honest, no one seriously doubts that it IS always true, but no one either has been able to prove it.

I was enjoying a lesson at St Philip Howard, one that was proving to be less painful than usual. The class included Jerry, a tiresome and thoughtless student who would constantly pester me for extra work (what a liberty!) I reached for Goldbach.

'Even, Jerry? You know what that means? Prime? Got the problem? Go away and explore.'

Three minutes later, Jerry came back with half a sheet of A4 covered in scribbles.

'It's obvious, sir, that Goldbach thing,' he said casually. 'I've proved it.'

Just for a moment, I wondered whether Jerry had proved it. I could see the photo on the front page of the *TES*, with Jerry holding a cheque for a million pounds while I stood with a fatherly arm around his shoulder, saying, 'That's my boy!' I inspected his proof with feverish anticipation, only to discover that Jerry's understanding of a prime number did not match with that of the wider mathematical community.

Goldbach's Conjecture is something of a misnomer. Goldbach's actual conjecture (in a letter to his friend, the mathematical superstar Euler) was that

'All whole numbers larger than 5 can be written as the sum of three primes.'

Euler replied that he preferred his version, that

'Every even number larger than 2 is the sum of two primes.'

Now this implies Goldbach's initial conjecture if it's true, but the reverse (mathematicians say 'the converse') is not true. Euler's version is called the Strong Goldbach Conjecture, while Goldbach's original conjecture is called the Weak one. (Clearly everyone felt that the ubiquitous Euler had had enough in the way of conjectures attributed to him.)

Rather extraordinarily, the Weak Goldbach Conjecture was proved in the course of writing this book, by Harald Helfgott in 2013. Tom, my Masters supervisor, rejoiced; "Fantastic that this should happen in my lifetime!" Perhaps it would've been fairer of me to set Jerry the Weak version. 'Now listen, sir, this really IS obvious…'

I remember a university talk where we students gave our lecturer, one of the top three number theorists in the world, a respectful silence. He was not, sadly, one of the top three mathematics communicators in the world, being a shy man who would clearly have been more at home working with a pencil and paper.

He'd decided to pass on to us news of a close attempt at proving the Strong Goldbach Conjecture, Chen Jingrun's stellar result of 1973 that every sufficiently large even number can be written either as the sum of two primes, or the sum of a prime and a semiprime (a semiprime is the product of exactly two primes, like $21 = 3 \times 7$).

'Every… sufficiently… large even number,' he ploughed on, unhappily wiping sweat from his brow, 'can be written either as the sum of two primes, or as the sum of a prime and another number…'

At this point, he paused for a much–needed sip of water. His audience were given just long enough to appreciate the achievement involved in proving this last 'theorem'. The lecture theatre collapsed into laughter and cheering, leaving our poor teacher completely baffled.

Far be it from me to defend such unkind behaviour (I can promise you that I wasn't laughing), but I feel sure that never can stopping for a glass of water have elicited such an impressive response. Maybe somewhere Goldbach and Euler were laughing too.

Liberation Mathematics Teaching

A shortage of vocations in the Roman Catholic Church in Latin America once meant that each priest was assigned an area the size of Belgium (maybe this is still true). What were the peasant communities to do whilst waiting for their turn to come around? They picked up their Bibles and started to read and discuss for themselves. As they did so, they produced a theology fresher and more authentic than anything their priests with their impressive academic backgrounds could create. So Liberation Theology was born.

Time for me to declare an interest; God means something to me. This is unfashionable these days. Many will say that the idea of God is an infantile father–fixation, a naïve wish–fulfilment. But for those who are agnostic about God, or who maybe believe in Him or Her, or who might even go far as to say they think they have encountered Him, I'd like to ask, 'What would a Liberation Theology of Mathematics Teaching look like?' My opening story suggests that whatever the answer, it can only be written by classroom mathematics teachers and learners themselves, rather than priestly theorists in universities who refuse to get their hands dirty.

My experience of learning mathematics as a young person was religious in its intensity. As teenagers in the Seventies, we didn't take ecstasy (it wasn't really around), but I'd have abstained; I had my mathematics. Even now, I'd say that my vision of God owes buckets to that time. On the one hand, God was transcendent, infinite, unknowable, truthful, absolute, yet on the other, knowable, intimate, powerful, friendly and good news. All of these ideas about God were paralleled in and strengthened through my experience of mathematics.

144

Let me take that word 'infinite'. What do most people think of when they hear this? The stars, the edge of the universe, and beyond? The urban myth tells us that the Inuit has many words for 'snow' – more truthfully, the mathematician has many for 'infinity'. When a mathematician hears God described as 'infinite', it sets off resonances in her imagination that are not always there for others, just as when water is eulogised at a baptism, a plumber may get a more visceral feeling for what is happening than will a mathematician.

I believe my life, whether I like it or not, is a theological statement, and that includes the way in which I earn my daily bread as a mathematics teacher. I try each day to make that statement as truthful and as beautiful as I can, and that is something that no one else can do for me.

The Promised Land

'Lord?'

'Yes, Jonny?'

'It's just that – as a maths teacher, I wish I was better organised.'

'I see. Tell me more.'

'It's just that my pile of *Things to be Sorted* never goes down. When it gets too big, I just pick it up and add it to another pile somewhere else.'

'Until the pile is too heavy to lift?'

'Exactly. Then I finish a day at College, and then I put a stack of papers into my bag, and then I get home, only to leave the bag untouched, saying, 'I'll deal with those in the morning when I get up at 5.30.' Then I get up at 6.30 and take the bag containing the papers, still untouched, back into College the next day. Then I repeat that five days a week.'

'Sounds like good exercise, if nothing else.'

'Then because I am so busy thinking about the papers in my bag, I'll press A4R rather than A4 on the photocopier without realising, and then press 222 rather than 22 without realising, and then I will save time by nipping to the loo while the copier is running...'

'Hmm. But doesn't every teacher need a reliable supply of scrap paper?'

'Then there's my lesson planning. Now I always spend half an hour planning every lesson, with at least five objectives, and timings to the nearest minute…'

'Jonny, you forget that I am omniscient.'

'Okay. But sometimes I do plan really carefully, and I know this lesson went brilliantly last year, and I <u>know</u> that I saved the sheet into that folder a year ago, but that is definitely the folder, and the sheet IS NOT IN THERE, and it MUST be a virus, there is no other explanation, and my students have started to come through the door...'

'So you wonder if you will ever make it to the Promised Land?'

'That's right! It's just that I can always see just ahead of me that day when I really do get organised, when no request for anything phases me, when I never have to pretend to the class that the reason I haven't marked that assignment is that I'm waiting for those three, okay, two, okay, that one outstanding piece to come in, when my graphics calculator possesses not a single mystery button, when tackling a Further Maths question blind I will always find the shortcut, when I touch every piece of paper just once, when...'

'Jonny, there is some good news, some bad news, and some really bad news.'

'I'll take the good news first.'

'The good news is that you will not be in this mess forever.'

'So I will reach the Promised Land! Thank you Lord! And the bad news?'

'The bad news is that like the Israelites, you will first spend forty years in the wilderness. And the really bad news is that your career will be exactly forty years long.'

Luke's Law

Philip, a bright but sloppy student a year and half into his A Level, offers me this in the course of a lesson.

'I need to solve $x^2 = 64$. It helps if I turn this into $x^2 - 64 = 0$, so I can use the quadratic formula with a = 1, b = -64 and c = 0. That gives me x is 0 or 64. Is that right?'

The quadratic formula is incredibly useful, but it's monstrous overkill to wheel it out for something as easy as $x^2 = 64$, and sadly, Philip has not even applied the formula properly. He tries to fathom why I'm weeping in a heap beneath the whiteboard.

As I wail, I recall that the master bridge player Eli Cuthbertson was once called upon in a court case. A husband and wife bridge pair had fallen out over a four spades contract that the poor woman had failed to make, whereupon her husband had shot her.

'I was able to offer in mitigation,' said Cuthbertson gravely, 'that on that hand, four spades was, in fact, possible.'

There are mistakes for which the weary teacher feels like clubbing (sorry) a student to a slow death. Are there errors so frightening that the teacher would walk away free from a subsequent trial?

Or perhaps it's not me who should be prosecuted, but Philip. I can see myself addressing the judge concerning his Grievously Bad Howler, as the young man stands unrepentant in the dock.

'Such a mistake, I humbly submit, your Honour, deserves life, and in this case, life should mean life.'

Yet… every student is innocent until proved guilty. My desire to brandish a red biro like St George's lance can be overhasty. A week later I'm marking Luke's work on elastic impact, and I come across this;

The reason for this is that

$$e = \frac{\textbf{\textit{angle of rebound}}}{\textbf{\textit{angle of incidence}}}$$

I've never seen anything like this before, and it brings me up short.

'This can't be true!' I murmur, and indeed, it gives completely the wrong answer. I write a challenging comment – 'You're busking, Luke!' – award no marks, and plough on. But something in his bravura niggles. I recall my mantra; 'There's no such thing as a silly mistake in my lesson.' Do I really believe that? I decide to bring up Luke's claim in a forgiving way next lesson.

'I wonder if we could examine Luke's Law for a minute.'

Ears perk up around the room. There's nothing students love more that the idea that one of their number might have come up with a new mathematical law that'll feature in textbooks for millennia to come, bringing its author a slice of immortality.

'Luke, how did you discover this?'

'To be honest, Jonny, it was a bit of a guess,' says Luke, surprising me with his frankness. 'But it just felt right.'

Intuition is not to be scorned in mathematics, and a little exploration revealed his premonition to be (almost) spot–on. This quantity e that Luke has been exploring is called the coefficient of restitution. It measures how bouncy the impact between two objects is. If the value of e for two balls is 1, then their impact is called perfectly elastic, and no energy is lost when they collide. If, however, the value of e is 0, then the two ball don't bounce off each other at all; they coalesce, and this time energy is certainly lost. Most impacts are somewhere in the middle, with e always lying between 0 and 1.

Another type of collision; oblique impact with a plane, as when a snooker ball bounces off one of the table's cushions.

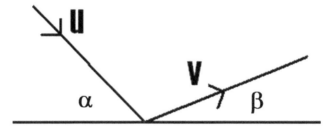

Here we split the motion into that parallel to the plane (where no energy is lost in the impact) and that perpendicular to the plane (where the collision will never be perfectly elastic).

That completely marvellous mathematician but rather miserable human being Newton came up with this law;

The speed of separation divided by the speed of approach equals e, the coefficient of restitution.

151

So perpendicular to the plane, we have $e = \dfrac{v \sin \beta}{u \sin \alpha}$, and parallel to the plane we have $u \cos \alpha = v \cos \beta$, and on combining these two equations, we have

$$e = \frac{\tan \beta}{\tan \alpha} \, .$$

By inserting two little tans, we tweak what Luke had surmised into something true, something that can happily bear the name Luke's Law without any grandiosity. We've also learnt a bit about elastic impact in the process.

So a student's technique may let them down, and they'll not always make four spades when four spades is possible. But sometimes they'll wing it, enjoy the chance to be intuitive, and make three spades instead – which is maybe something to be celebrated?

You Have a Go

Gavin, one of my fellow-teachers at St Philip Howard, looked up as I walked into my classroom, and we exchanged hellos. He'd just finished teaching a lesson there, and was now leafing through a book that I'd left on my table called *Teaching Algebra*. Its author was Malcolm Rogers, a prolific writer in the maths education field.

'Are you a fan then?' I asked. To be honest, I was surprised to see him looking at such a book. Gavin's lessons had a reputation for being 'traditional' – his students sat rapt in awe of his knowledge, but never really formed a close bond. 'The Iceman' was his nickname. So why was Gavin reading my improving book?

'A fan, Jonny? Of Malcolm Rogers?' He sat down, tossing the book to one side. He appeared upset about something. 'I should think so. Look, we teach in an inner city comprehensive, do we not?'

I nodded.

'Your friend Mr Rogers – has he ever been through what we go through, I wonder?' Gavin paused, letting a little of his anger go in a sigh.

'I know the man. When I started my teaching career in a Birmingham comp, Malcolm Rogers was the area's Chief Inspector for Mathematics. He'd never taught in a school, or even a college. University only.'

I said nothing, as Gavin stared at me, clearly reliving a painful memory.

'He had some hard things to say about departments in some schools. And as he walked out the gates, those teachers would roll their eyes and say, "I know! Why don't you have a go, mate!" '

I wondered what Malcolm Rogers had said about Gavin's teaching.

'Oh, he knew his stuff, he was a committed educationalist, he cared about the young people he was responsible for. But in the job itself, Jonny,' he added, 'he wouldn't have lasted ten minutes.'

Gavin stopped speaking, his anger causing him to shake a little. I felt a real concern for my colleague. This was not 'The Iceman', rather 'The Towering Inferno'.

'But isn't there room for all sorts in maths education?' I asked. 'Don't we teachers need the theorists and don't the theorists need us?'

'I've got time for those who teach kids,' said Gavin, calmer now, 'and I've got time for those who aspire to teach kids. I've also got time for those who have left the classroom but who secretly wish they could go back.' He blew his nose. 'But I don't have time for people who would rather write a maths teaching book than do any maths teaching themselves.'

'But Gavin,' I urged, feeling angry myself now. 'You come across great football managers who were fairly ordinary footballers. Can't you imagine someone who is not cut out to be a teacher, but who's perfectly cut out to be a theoriser about teaching?'

Gavin stood and made for the corridor. 'Those football managers at least had a go, Jonny,' he said, calmly now. 'Enjoy your book.'

154

Who Taught Me That?

Marking the other day, I chance across this, in a disorganised script by a student called Jack:

I stop, puzzled. Did Jack need a diversion midway through his tough trigonometry assignment, and turn to draft a love letter to his lucky inamorata? But then I work it out– Jack's intention was to write this:

So Jack was writing his Letter–xs and his Times–xs in the same way. I think back, and dimly recall a time when I did the same - maybe forty years past? Who was it who'd passed on the wisdom that Letter–xs were better written as two semi–circles? The effort of memory is too great, but in any case, I silently thank the ubiquitous teacher Anon.

Was there anything comparable in my mathematical makeup? I think of the numeral 7 – I always put a line through it, to differentiate it from the digit 1, and likewise with my Letter–z (to distinguish it from 2). But these foibles seemed to me more optional than writing a Letter–x with two half–circles. I drew up the following Venn diagram:

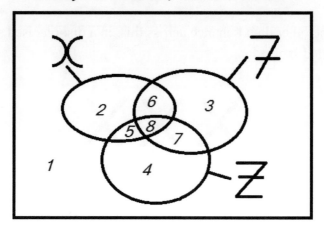

I found myself positioned squarely in region 8; where would my students be? Studying Jack's homework placed him in region 1, and I would gently suggest next time that he migrated into the x–as–two–half–circles bubble at least.

The next time I have the group, I do a survey. We have lots of x–as–two–half–circles ('We were taught that at primary school!'), a smattering of seven–with–a–line people, while I'm almost on my own with my z–with–a–dash option.

What's second nature is hard to question. I'm not sure in twenty years I've ever stopped to consider that how to write the letter x deserves at least ten seconds of the A Level course. It makes me wonder – what other symbols do I use without stopping to bring everyone on board? Why on earth have I not explored this before? It seems a blindingly obvious thing for a teacher to try to explain.

When I ask, my students are keen to help. It transpires I abbreviate 'positive' to $+ve$ and 'negative' to $-ve$, mysterious until you crack it. The vast majority do, but those who skip it without asking, thinking 'Jonny will explain that in a minute', are disappointed. Then a symbol that could have been my own invention:

Well, 'perpendicular' is such a mouthful. But do I stop to explain this to every class I teach, every time? In the heat of a difficult day with a mind juggling ten different jobs at a time, I know I don't. How about RHS and LHS, for the 'right-hand side' and the 'left hand side' of an equation; these clearly need to be decoded. Then there is my cheery but potentially unhelpful version of the ampersand, as in

This looks like the Greek letter gamma, so I could in theory end up writing 'gamma and delta' as the impossibly cryptic

$$\gamma \ \gamma \ \delta$$

I sigh, and once again try to dredge up a moral for myself from this cautionary tale. The best I can do is this; firstly, may I be grateful to those teachers who once upon a time improved my mathematics in ways that stay with me, but who are long forgotten. But secondly, if I fail to put myself into my students' shoes, it's unlikely that anyone will do this for me.

Cruise Control

When I made the move to a Sixth Form College, most of my discipline problems melted away. The magic phrase, 'They've chosen to be here,' made all the difference. Those five words created a dynamic that suited me; my students and I were adults together, wearing whatever we wanted and on first name terms. Discipline problems in an SFC do exist; I've taught GCSE resit classes there, and they contain some decidedly rough diamonds. Sometimes even an A Level class can contain individuals who are a headache. But mostly, we were blessedly free to get on.

Eventually I arrived at a formula for classroom discipline, a 'Three strikes and you're out' system. Be a pain once, I give you a warning. Twice, and I move you to the front, somewhere far from your friends. Three times, and I ask you to leave (given that everyone was 16 or over, I could always ask anyone unhelpfully hyperactive to head off to the cafe to cool down). We'll then get together to discuss things with your tutor. My system was eventually automatic, and not in the least bit personal.

The curious paradox was that once I had this system in place, and was clear in my own mind over how to apply it, I didn't need it any more. When I retired, it'd been years since I'd sent a student out. Margaret back in Tower Hamlets had a hard edge to her discipline, but because it was there, she only rarely needed to resort to it.

At Paston, I called upon signs to help me. With these, a simple point of the finger can be enough to puncture misbehaviour. The more cryptic ones lead to an instructional guessing game for newcomers, while signs suggested from the floor can always be considered. Here are the ones that proved to be most useful:

Three strikes and you're out.

No tipping of seats.

No eating (doubling up as no yo–yos).

Questions encouraged (it's important to have some positive signs).

My intention for this sign was 'No arguing with the ref!' My students' reading of this sign was 'No singing of YMCA.'

My students tended to pack away noisily as soon as I started to set homework. Thus the need for this sign; no rustling.

On one occasion, I saw Robbie and Ben working furiously hard together. Now there are grades of activity in a classroom; there's slacking (not good), working hard (good) and there's working surprisingly hard (maybe very good, but possibly suspicious). It transpired they were busy sign–creating. The result was this;

A sign banning all signs that ban things. That made me think; how about this?

A new rule: a sign that doesn't ban itself has a grey border.

Which means that this must be a sign banning all signs that don't ban themselves.

Now we have a problem. Should the outside border be black or grey?

If it's grey, then it should be black, and if it is black, then it should be grey.

Kurt Godel proved a famous theorem in 1930, telling us that in any mathematical system complicated enough to include arithmetic there will always be true results that can't be proved, which at the time was something of a body blow for mathematics. How did he manage this? He employed at the heart of his proof a contradiction similar to the one above. I hope he would he chuffed to see his monumental theorem summed up by a single innocent-looking sign on a classroom wall.

Sprouts

Sometimes a student says something so smart and sweet that you just have to stand back and let the tears roll down your cheeks, even though she's made you look mighty foolish.

I'm playing the game of Sprouts with my class. It's a fun way to get into the science of drawing dots with connecting lines (mathematicians call this 'graph theory').

The rules are these; draw a small number of dots on a page. Now take it in turns with a partner to draw lines connecting dots, so that when you connect two dots with a line, you place another dot at the middle of the line. Lines cannot cross! The extra rules are these; once a dot has three lines coming out of it, it's dead and can't be used again, and the winner is the last person to draw a legal line.

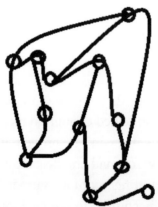

The diagram above shows a completed game starting with four dots. The origin of the name of the game is up for debate, but I say it's since the resulting diagram looks like an overcooked Brussels sprout. It was invented by Michael S. Paterson and John Horton Conway in the 1960s.

164

I use the game to introduce Euler's Theorem (this time Euler does get to name the result). This says that in the final diagram (assuming this is connected, which means you can travel from any dot to any other along connecting lines) the number of dots (V for vertices) plus the number of regions (F for faces) minus the number of connecting lines (E for edges) is always 2 (try it!).

$$V + F - E = 2.$$

You need to count the outside region as a face for this to work. A completed Sprouts game, if counted carefully afterwards, will show that this law holds for that graph. For the diagram above, $V = 12$, $F = 6$.and $E = 16$, and $V + F - E = 2$.

I sense the game goes well enough, although Eleanor looks troubled throughout. Once everyone has added up, I ask innocently, 'So why do you think the game's called Sprouts?

Eleanor comes straight back with, 'Because nobody liked it.'

Hilarity ensues, and I am included. But later I pick up an email saying that Eleanor is suffering from depression and needs a compassionate approach. Was her sharp comment trying to communicate something?

Red Nose Day

Schools like to align themselves with charities, and Red Nose Day is no exception. 'Come in fancy dress for a pound!' The kids rejoice at the chance to cast off their uniforms, while mature teachers brace themselves for a day where pupils will be higher than usual ('high' is a teacher word for 'wild'; kids are higher in the afternoon than the morning, and also when there is rain and wind around.)

So St Philip Howard aimed to put on a good show. Teachers were expected to come in character, which led me to survey my wardrobe. A leftover from my performing days, I still had a bright red check jacket, together with trousers that were even louder.

'I'll go in as a clown', I thought. A sense of foreboding skittered across my mind.

I constructed a lesson to match about polygons. A polygon is a shape with straight line sides. A regular polygon has all sides equal and all angles equal (a square is one example, a rectangle is not). If you ask yourself to build a solid using just a single regular polygon, copied as many times as you like, your options are limited. It transpires that there are five solids that obey this rule, as found by Plato; the tetrahedron (four equilateral triangles), the cube (six squares), the octahedron (eight equilateral triangles), the dodecahedron (twelve regular pentagons) and the icosahedron (twenty equilateral triangles).

The finished icosahedron is close to being a sphere, and I planned to get each of my class to make one of these from red paper, to wear as a red nose. Now there are dangers here; we can imagine an unholy muddle of glue and scissors, a near-guarantee of disaster in the hands of twelve-year-olds. Here is where I cunningly removed the glue worry, at least; we would plait our icosahedrons. Remarkably, it's possible to cut from a single sheet of A4 a single net with three strands that when carefully creased and plaited give you a perfect icosahedron, with no glue or sellotape needed – the final flap tucks in neatly. To start with, **o**(ver) goes over **u**(nder).

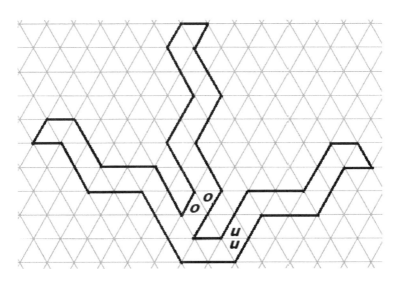

167

The lesson in my mind featured happy, curious students absorbed by the demanding (yet not too demanding) task, and indeed, the start went swimmingly, with curiosity and industry combining well. There was the gentle hum of students cutting and folding, and I congratulated myself on hitting the mark. But then my pupils ran into a wall.

'These scissors are useless!'

'No, that doesn't fold over that, you moron!'

'I've just chopped off one of my bits, what do I do now?'

They were finding the work too intricate. It's sometimes said teachers should have higher expectations of their students; I sometimes feel my expectations have been way too high, with every student, for every lesson I've ever taught.

'This is really, honestly,' my insides scream from time to time, 'a piece of cake, why are you finding it so hard?'

The cutting out here asked for precision that my pupils could not deliver, the creasing needed a light touch that it turned out my ham-fisted charges could only dream about, and once the cutting and creasing went wrong, the plaiting had no chance. I was now half-way through the lesson, with no back-up plan, and noise levels were heading through the roof. I desperately tried to help a group of three students with their plait, only to hear a shout behind me. I turned to see John doing a dervish dance while standing on his chair. I felt sick; this was wildness that was off the scale.

'Get down, John, you idiot,' I cried in alarm. A moment later he decided to leap to the floor. He made a terrible fist of this, catching his knee on a table.

'Ooooow!' he yelled, lying on the floor. He pulled up a trouser leg to reveal a lump of flesh hanging precariously from his body.

'Oh, my God!' cried the class as one, as if we'd just reached the climax of some horror B-movie.

'Do something!' Sandra shouted at me.

'HE doesn't know what to do!' said Shahid.

'Get Sue from next door!' I cried. *Surely*, I thought crazily, *in my first year I'm allowed to pass the buck.*

Calling Sue proved to be a bright move. Suddenly things scorched along. John's parents were summoned, an ambulance turned up, and Paula, my Head, arrived and entered bomb defusal mode, skilfully playing down the whole incident.

'Mr and Mrs Masters, let me introduce you to Mr Griffiths, John's maths teacher!' she enthused, flashing me a broad smile.

Still in my clown's outfit, I slowly leant forward and shook hands with a wan grin.

'My exploding car is outside,' I said gamely. No one laughed.

You Shouldn't Have Said That

'What do we call a line that just touches a circle?' I ask my GCSE resit class.

'Gay?' replies Rob, all wide-eyed innocence.

As it has elsewhere, the word 'gay' has developed an all-purpose meaning at our college. 'This lunch is gay,' 'Your pencil box is gay,' 'That's a gay thing to say.' It rough translates as 'daft,' or even 'crap.' Does it have homophobic undertones? It is hard to see how it cannot.

In previous lessons, Rob has projected an image of himself as, well, more than comfortable with his heterosexuality, let's say. How to reply?

There are two reactions that I think won't wash. The first is to do and say nothing. Stonewall have documented the appalling suffering gay students can be made to endure in schools and colleges, and as a teacher, I wish to place myself firmly on the side of such students.

The second is to start wheeling in heavy-duty college policies and disciplinary procedures, which clearly have their place, but not as a response to this kind of skittish wind-up. Rather than something suffocatingly earnest, a light but pointed response is needed. How about:

'Rob, are you saying that straight lines are better than gay ones?'

Sadly, I thought of this afterwards (damn!), so Rob's reply cannot be recorded (just as well, possibly).

It's worth noting that Rob's remark arose out of the mathematics itself. Here is a similar incident taken from an upper sixth Mechanics group lesson about calculus:

'Differentiation is a science, while integration is an art,' I say. 'You can differentiate any standard function; there are clear rules. When it comes to integration, however, the rules are less cut and dried. There are standard functions you can't integrate.'

Isaac laughs. 'That's because integration was invented by a woman,' he says, and the others (all boys) laugh too.

'Do you mean that, Isaac?' I ask.

He looks dismissive. 'I was just being ironic, Jonny,' he says. 'A little post-modern.'

Something I'd said myself to the group a little earlier in the term (damn!).

I later relate this story in the staff-room, and my colleagues (both men and women) think Isaac's remark is great fun. But Brigid, a maths colleague, had reservations.

'I took that group when you were out the other day, and there's a misogynistic streak in there,' she says. 'They didn't like being taught by a woman.'

For her, Isaac's banter was a pointer to a genuine, albeit unconscious, problem within the group. Suppose one girl had decided to take the Mechanics option? Would Isaac have said what he did, would I have reacted differently? Maybe the story shows why not a single girl took the course.

What a minefield. Society's mixed up over sexism and sexuality, so my classroom will be too. How would you counter this conversation?

Three girls are whispering together.

(Girl 1) 'So then she called her a lesbian!'
(Girl 2) 'No!'
(Girl 3) 'What's wrong with being a lesbian?'

I butt in: 'There's nothing wrong with being a lesbian, but this is not a break. At the moment, maths is all you are allowed to talk about!'

Brief pause: (Girl 1) 'So, how many lesbians does it take...'

Invigilation Poetry

Box them in, tie them down, oversee with teacher frown,
Searching for the prying-eyed - woe to those who quick-revised!

I'm walking the aisles of our gym, watching this year's set of young hopefuls tackle their GCSE resit maths paper. As I take in the surreal sight of my students all working on mathematics simultaneously in complete silence, I wonder how best to fill my invigilation time. I need to be at least moderately alert and watchful, so most useful activities are out. Playing *Slow-motion Tag* with the other invigilators palls after a while. Which leaves composing poems about the exam process in my head.

The paper's packaged by a team, honed and polished, questions gleam,
Wrenching knowledge from the ground, pulling roots without a sound.

I enjoy watching students arranging their kit on the exam table as they start. Some go for the minimalist approach, displaying just their ID card and a biro, while others look as if they are planning to open a stationery shop halfway through the paper. Some dump their bits and pieces into a random pile, while others arrange their exam technology like a sacristan laying out bread and wine. I am surprised today to see a girl with a protractor on her desk – for a Film Studies exam. Maybe she's hoping for this:

'Kurosawa's *Ran* **could be viewed as Oriental Film Noir.'**
Discuss this angle on the film.

Students caught hook line and sinker,
Heads on hands, like Rodin's thinker,

173

Invigilator joins in fully,
Acquiescing to be bully.

Exam season can be worse for the teachers than for students. I caught sight of our Exams Officer the other day, walking towards an A Level maths exam with a pile of log tables. A sudden terror seized my mind – were log tables back on the syllabus, and would my students be completely at sea since I'd given them no practice at all in their use?

'What are they for, Sam?' I asked. To my relief, he said, 'We stick them under the tables to stop them wobbling.' The incident made me reflect on how everything, but everything, becomes obsolete eventually. In ten years' time, we may well be sellotaping six graphics calculators together and using them as a doorstop.

No-one questions question time, all accept the nursery rhyme,
'Good boys and girls come out to play, after scoring well today.'

Some educationalists divide mathematical pedagogues into Exam-Results Teachers and Love-of-Maths Teachers. I would hope I am first and foremost the latter, but the truth is that these days every serious teacher has to be both. Which does not mean that a little healthy scepticism about the whole rigmarole of exams is forbidden.

And those who don't? Well, they'll try too,
None can think what else to do,
This might be different, and besides,
You play the game, or woe betides...

174

Red Nose Day II

Paula directed me to see John and his parents off the premises. Feeling haggard, worrying about John, and cursing myself for teaching an unrealistic lesson, I headed to the main hall of the school, still shamelessly wearing my garish outfit. The entire school would be crammed in now, for a debrief on how the day had gone.

There was a brief talent contest of sorts, with aged pianos hammered and cheap guitars thrashed, which ended with Paula standing to address the group. She looked out onto a sea of wild kids, pushing and chatting and laughing now that the journey home was in sight.

'She's not going to try that, is she?' muttered Chris, the geography teacher standing next to me. For Paula had set herself the challenge of quelling the entire hall whilst still wearing her red nose. 'My God, she is.'

She stood, feet planted squarely on the stage floorboards, and a quieting force seemed to emanate from her body. The front row felt it first, but it swiftly spread five rows back, and then ten, subduing whilst commanding. I squinted - was her nose glowing? It wasn't, but it might as well have been. The effect of Paula's authority was magical. It took ninety seconds, but she instilled absolute quiet into her rough audience.

'Well done to you all,' she said calmly, her nose bobbing like a tiny red buoy in choppy waves. There was no triumphalism. 'It's been a great day, with £2 000 raised! Be careful on the way home! Back row first!'

And with that, she handed things over to her staff, popped off her nose, and presumably with next year in mind, pushed it into a pocket.

Maths is Beautiful

Bertrand Russell was a man of many parts - philosopher, anti-war activist, logician, prisoner for his beliefs, historian, Nobel Laureate and more. He once said:

Mathematics possesses a beauty cold and austere, sublimely pure, and capable of a stern perfection such as only the greatest art can show.

Most people would shake their heads at this. Their encounters with mathematics lead them to argue maths is painful, rather than beautiful. 'What does this mathematical beauty look like?' I hear. It's a fair question. If it can only be appreciated by professors like Russell, then it seems a touch elitist.

Let me propose a game. Imagine that you have nine cards bearing the digits 1 to 9 lying on the table in front of you.

You and a friend take it in turns to pick a card. The winner is the first person to have exactly three cards in their hand that add up to 15. If you have a moment, find a companion and play this game a few times, to get the feel for it.

A sample game might go like this:

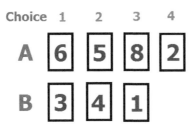

Player B is forced to pick 4 as their second choice to block A from getting 6–5–4, but then A is forced in turn to block Player B by picking 8. Player B is then in an impossible dilemma; he has to pick both 1 and 2 to block A, and so he loses – B picks 1, and Player A ends with the winning combination 2–5–8 in their hand.

A bagatelle to while away a minute, you might think, but a mathematician drawn into this will be asking questions. Is it better to go first or second? Is it guaranteed that with best strategy the game will end in a win for one side or the other, or is a draw possible? What is this best strategy? What if the game has more cards, and what if the target number 15 can vary? How about a three–player version? Generalising, extending, varying, these are all things that a mathematician does. She asks, 'How can I look at this in a different way?'

Perhaps, even, in a more beautiful way.

Suppose our mathematician picks the cards up and rearranges them on the table. 'The numbers from 1 to 9, and the number 15,' she reflects, triggering a memory. She places the nine cards like this:

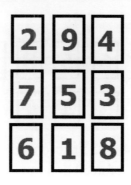

'Each row adds to 15, each column adds to 15, and each of the main diagonals adds to 15. The game asks me to pick three cards that add to 15 – in other words, I am trying to get a line of three.'

Suddenly it dawns - the game is in fact Noughts and Crosses. All the questions about strategy are resolved, since we've all played Noughts and Crosses a thousand times; with best play, the game should always end in a draw, although if you are playing an inexperienced player, it does help to go first.

Translating our sample game into Noughts–and–Crosses–speak helps us to appreciate the sample game I gave you above and Player B's problem more keenly.

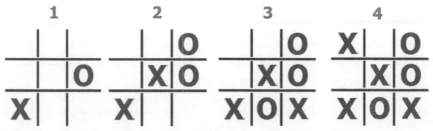

There is one check we need to make; is EVERY way of making 15 with three cards represented in our magic square? Research shows the

178

answer is 'Yes'. There are exactly eight different ways of making 15 with three different cards, and there are exactly eight different ways shown in our magic square. The analogy is perfect, and the underlying structure for these two games that initially look different is seen to be identical.

Mathematicians love to find similar structure in different situations; they would describe the two games as 'isomorphic'. Spotting an isomorphism saves you work. Insights concerning the first side of the isomorphism cross over into understandings concerning the second, and vice versa.

So the argument above takes an unfamiliar game and helps us realise that is in fact a familiar one. What is it that enchants me about this logic? We start with something one–dimensional (a line of cards), and turn it into something two–dimensional (a magic square of cards). Maybe I feel a slight uneasiness playing the initial game ('something tells me I've seen this before...') which is then sweetly resolved by the magic square arrangement.

Then there's the precision of the fact that there are exactly eight ways to get three cards to add to 15, and there are exactly eight ways to read 15 from the magic square. If you try the game with 16 cards from 1 to 16 and a 4 by 4 magic square, the isomorphism breaks down. In fact, the argument is so fragile, which is part of its beauty. Change the number 15 to 14 or 16, and the logic evaporates.

Now that I have seen this beautiful magic square trick, I have a new implement for my mathematical toolbox. Whenever I see a problem that reminds me of this one, I'll ask if this method could be used. And of

179

course, magic squares of various sizes have a rich history of their own too.

It may be that you like this game and its resolution, but you don't count it as maths. So firmly is the law, 'Maths is not Fun!' embedded in your psyche that anything enjoyable is by definition unmathematical. If I describe you here, maybe your vision of maths needs widening.

It may be that this solution to finding the game's best strategy does nothing for you. I recall a story about a woman who asked Fats Waller what jazz was. 'If you have to ask, you'll never know!' was his reply. Those unaffected by this game may feel even angry; *time spent on nothing, while true sources of beauty like poetry, art and music are ignored.*

My reply would be that no mathematician claims that their appreciation of beauty trumps anybody else's. Whether it's a chemist contemplating the benzene ring, or an economist reflecting on the most worthwhile way to set up a company, or an extraordinary piece of sport or poetry or art, to set up a competition between our respective beauties would be ugly in the extreme.

For every teacher the question should be the same, 'How can I pass on beauty?' I gazed out each year at my new groups, and wondered about their prior experience. 'How many will have chosen to pursue the beauty of maths beyond the syllabus in their spare time?' The percentage was small. 'How could I increase it?'

There's plenty of mathematics that's more immediately useful than aesthetic, yet in the right hands, beauty can be found even here. Apparent drudgery can be approached in a multitude of ways, some of which acknowledge beauty more than others. As the great mathematician Gauss once said, 'You have no idea how much poetry there is in the calculation of a table of logarithms!'

There's a moment in Simon Singh's already-mentioned masterpiece on Fermat's Last Theorem when Andrew Wiles tries to communicate the experience of finding the final piece of the jigsaw. This gentle man sits on film for maybe fifteen seconds in complete silence as he grapples with the enormity of the vision granted to him. It's as if at that point he reached the mountain top, to gaze out into a virgin valley beyond that he'd completely subdued through the lonely power of his fallible human mind.

'It was so indescribably beautiful', he says quietly, like Moses attempting to describe meeting God in the burning bush.
Maybe in the end it's only the spiritual that suffices to talk of any perception of beauty. Okay, I'm a theist (although I concede I might be wrong), but there are plenty of atheists out there leading profoundly spiritual lives who I hope would agree.

I was an idealistic teacher. I wanted to initiate my classes into the human conversation that is mathematics, taking the appreciation of mathematical beauty as our cornerstone. I wanted us to be able to look back at our hours in my classroom together as a time of wonder. Maybe not non–stop wonder, for that would be too much to bear, but if possible, our brief moments of transcendence would be remembered.

My old colleagues, if they are reading this, will smile. My ideals did not make it into practice every day. I would foolishly tell my students in advance, 'Now here's a beautiful piece of maths coming,' only to be met afterwards by blank faces; 'Was that it?'

181

My students learnt that I looked for 'elegance' in mathematics; they would mischievously raise their hand after seeing a smart solution and ask, 'Would you say that that was (ahem) "elegant", Jonny?' Well, yes, my friends, I would, and I count myself blessed to think so. I love to think that one day, you will too.

Front Row, Back Row

There are two kinds of students in my Paston classroom, front row students and back row students. They are, I hardly need to say, different animals.

Front row students are always on time, have excellent powers of concentration, and have sensible hair-cuts. At the end of a lesson, I can easily imagine a front row student giving me an apple.

Back row students, on the other hand, drift off task, are more likely to be rocking on their chairs, and have a fascination with their own knees. It's almost as if they're texting under the table, but I know no student of mine would ever do that; it must just be that they have really nice knees.

This is the Montagues and Capulets all over again. Occasionally a front row girl goes out with a back row boy, but it's always doomed.

The severest punishment I have available to me is to ask, just for a while, for a back row boy to become a front row boy.

'No please, Jonny, anything but that... '

Raja's the most front row of front row students, bang in the middle. His levels of concentration are frightening. Now I must confess that occasionally as a maths teacher you think up at the board;

'Blimey that's interesting, I wonder if...'

183

At this point you go into a little trance (or is that just me?) At such times I can always feel Raja's eyes boring into my back, saying,

'Hey, Jonny, we're here too...'

Jacob, on the other hand, is that rare creature, a back row boy with a front row mentality. He therefore manages to combine being good at maths with being cool at the same time, a formula that's sadly escaped me for over forty years.

Ellie

Ellie was a quiet girl, maybe even diffident. Her maths was, well, all right, I thought, for a further mathematician.

Maybe in my arrogance I placed unconscious limits on my expectations, and Ellie's final A Level results did not set the world on fire.

She left our college, and dropped off my radar. But then, ten years later, I took on a Masters at my local university.

I knew Ellie had pitched up there to study maths; it transpired that she'd been awarded a first, coming top in her year, and that she'd gone on to complete a highly successful PhD.

My supervisor had looked after Ellie as well as myself, and he spoke in hushed tones about the import of her main theorem.

By coincidence, I was researching into the same areas Ellie had explored, and I was able to look at her results.

She was now teaching me, and I struggled to grasp her words – in fact, they were way beyond me.

Did I hear Ellie gently asking, 'Whose maths is, well, all right, now, Jonny?'

The Madhouse

It was the close of my second term in the East End. I was teaching in my room when the door opened, and a student I didn't know ran in. Before I could say a word, a second student followed him into the room. The first incomer ran over to my window, and jumped out, closely followed by the second student. My class carried on as through nothing had happened. Was this normal? As I watched the school in action day by day, these mad events came to seem routine.

I taught on the first floor, above a long-suffering colleague called Sister Alison. In my mind she'd swiftly developed an unofficial barometer for assessing the state of my lessons; if she saw bits of paper fluttering down, that was a placid day, if textbooks came down, the waters were choppy, and if students came down, thunder and lightning were crashing overhead. At this point she would be a Sister of Mercy and press a secret panic button through to management, which led to one of the hierarchy popping their head around my door.

For One World Week I decided to try a lesson suggested by the World Development Movement. Each table in the room would role-play a nation, which began with a mix of technology (compasses, rulers and scissors) and raw materials (various pieces of paper in various colours). The majority of tables possessed lots of raw materials but little technology, while the elite few possessed technology but were much in need of raw materials.

When I clapped loudly to start the game, two activities were allowed; the drawing and cutting out of goods (circles, triangles and squares), and trading (the swapping of technology and raw materials between tables). When I clapped loudly to end the game, the value of the goods

186

created would be totted up for each country and a winner would be declared. 'The game should last an hour' was the advice.

You can see the idea; pupils would pick up from this that the world order is unfairly skewed. But asking my Tower Hamlets crew to appreciate any idea of unfairness without fisticuffs was deranged. The room volume went through the roof, war broke out between three different pairs of nations, and goods and technology were shamelessly stolen from neighbouring tables (rather too much like real life then). Sister Alison must have been thumping her panic button with a crazy urgency, as three members of the senior management team arrived simultaneously. I shouted out to end the trading; the activity had lasted less than ten minutes. A look round the room showed nothing in the way of circles, triangles or squares sitting neatly on tables, rather a confetti of paper shreds on the floor through which pupils shuffled as they travelled back to their seats. I gave a cheery 'That went just as I'd hoped!' smile to my senior colleagues, and then tried to cobble together some kind of lesson for the remaining forty minutes.

More madness. Those sitting on a table together would from time to time mount a cussing competition. Taking a pair of scissors from their shared tray, they would spin it on the table. Whoever the scissors eventually pointed at would have to cuss one of the other members of the group without pause for breath. The least imaginative of these cusses was to say, 'Yer mum,' which was apparently short for 'Your mum's a whore.' This could only be topped by 'Yer nan'. This vacuous and misogynistic game could occupy students happily for hours. The ideal of maternal purity was a strong thread for all my students. If a student wanted you to trust them on something, they would look into your eyes and say, 'On my mother's honour, Sir. I can't say more than that.'

187

The craziness was not confined to my lessons. Lazlo, a Polish kid in his GCSE year, brought in an airgun one day, and started firing off at people in the playground from an upstairs window. He was thankfully a lousy shot, and his pellets safely missed their targets. He then opened the window further, and while standing on the ledge, threatened to throw himself off. Paula, my Head, was in the classroom with Lazlo as I got there, talking the troubled lad round. She got near enough to make a grab, and Lazlo found himself back indoors.

The occasional psychotic kid was only one aspect of the job. Additional pressure came from parents, who often seemed to think we teachers were all overpaid freeloaders. The younger staff would slip way to the pub down the road at the end of the day, to meet glares from the regulars. A charity collection would be hastily invented ('Let's see how much those sodding teachers give…').

Some of the staff were no saner than either the parents or their children. Brian, my Head Tutor, a selfless and committed practitioner, was dangerously close to the edge. My form had their assembly on a Friday with six others. Strictly speaking, the form tutors had to accompany their tutees, but it was a well-worn dodge to leave it to the others and catch up with marking. On this Friday, I was the only teacher out of seven to materialise. Brian's day had seen unacceptable stress levels, and this was the final insult. He began to rant at the kids.

'And you know what, this is the fifth week running that I have been poorly served by staff!' he shouted.

Brian was beyond considering how I might feel - I clearly didn't count as a teacher in his reckoning. The kids sat in silence, unsure what to make of this. They were used to being raged at in assemblies, but to be on the end of a tongue-lashing aimed at teachers was a first.

'There's no doubt,' I thought, as Brian shrieked towards break, 'this is a mighty curious school where people are pushed into doing mighty curious things.'

The Special Teacher

Once there was young man who loved both mathematics and people. 'How about a career in teaching?' he wondered. 'I want to give something back.'

So that's what he did. It took him a while, but in time he found the right place. He put down roots and committed himself to these colleagues and these students.

He worked hard at his teaching. His lessons were well–prepared, he did plenty of marking, and his reports were incisive. His fellow–teachers saw him as a safe pair of hands, one of the rocks on which the school could be built.

His students loved him and the mathematics they studied together. They were not all high–fliers (some found mathematics hard), but they sensed the man cared for them all equally, celebrating the weaker students' achievements as much as those who won A grades.

The man's work was noted more widely. His resources made their way into classrooms nationally. His articles drew praise from people in the know. He was asked to lead sessions at conferences, and then days at conferences. He began to breathe a different air to his colleagues back in his school. Without fully realising what was happening, the man began to hear the words, 'You're a special teacher,' whispered into his ear.

He signed up for courses like, 'Inspirational Mathematics Leadership for the Twenty–First Century', courses that required missing many days of teaching time. Whenever he was away on yet one more day, his students missed him. They were taken instead by a supply teacher who didn't really know them, and as they settled to work on tasks that felt foreign they became resentful.

'He used to care about us,' they thought, 'but now he cares more about other things.'

A change took place; they stopped understanding the man. He'd always prided himself on his explanations, but his students ceased to value them.

'He used to explain the maths, but now he just tells us what it is.'

The same words, in the same order, but with a different result, because his heart was elsewhere.

Parents grew unhappy, tutors grew fearful, his results got poorer. One day, the man took stock.

'I've forgotten my roots,' he thought. 'I was once a teacher planted firmly in my own classroom, but now I've lost my earthiness. I've been seduced; I must start again.'

So the man cancelled all his conferences, and he shelved his article-writing. He walked back into his classroom with a fresh spirit of humility. His students were glad to see him, and they started to understand him again. And although the man did one day go back to writing and speaking, he never again forgot the reason that he went into teaching in the first place, He never again lost his ordinariness.

Stress Test

I'm up at the board with my second year A Level group, at the end of what's been a demanding week. Reports were due yesterday, and as usual management have been sparked into accusatory emails over spelling mistakes and grammar.

'There is a difference between "practice" and "practise," ' rages Ralph, our deputy head. I feel I know him well enough after twenty years to email back.

'Couldn't agree more, Ralph, we should certainly practice what we preach,' preparing as I do so to be put gently in my place at lunchtime.

I do sometimes makes errors in my reports that are worrying – I remember mistakenly cutting and pasting Jeremy a target to 'make sure you look after your health in the months ahead.' I usually aim this at students who've been absent for a range of minor 'ailments', some of which are their own fault (like hangovers), but in this case Jeremy had not missed a lesson and had been the epitome of sanguine youthfulness. With that background, my target became impressively sinister, as if I were a mafia boss who knew something ominous about Jeremy's immediate future. Luckily Jeremy was puzzled enough to raise it with me.

So reports came this week on top of the normal routine, and an extra and unexpected meeting this morning has additionally drained my resources. Through half-open eyes, I crack on with some calculus.

'So we take the derivative…' I write $\dfrac{dy}{dx}$ on the board.

Chris sticks up an arm straight away. He looks considerably more alert than I feel.

'Shouldn't that dx be a dt, Jonny?'

I peer at the board, a quiet headache pulsing.

'Yes, Chris, thank you.' I make the alteration, only to see another hand skyward. Caroline this time, wearing a wicked grin.

'And shouldn't the dy be a dx?'

'Er… yes, well spotted again, Caroline, thank you.'

Laughter erupts around the room. To get the top AND bottom of a derivative wrong is as bad as it gets. I have to take this ribbing ruefully on the chin.

As the hilarity subsides, Briony says, 'The ds were good, though, Jonny.'

Derivatives

Sean is up at the board.

'So

$$\frac{dy}{dx} = y'$$

?'

'That's right,' I say.

'And

$$\frac{d^2y}{dx^2} = y''$$

?'

'That's right again,' I say.

'So does

$$\frac{d^5y}{dx^5} = y^{\text{卌}}$$

?'

Golden Boy

The gym is packed. I take a sip of my rough powered coffee and reflect that I (usually) enjoy Parents' Evening. Sometimes you find yourself forgiving a student much once you've met their parents. Of course, it tends to be the good students and their proud fathers and mothers who turn up in the main, and it's a great pleasure to be able to praise from the heart those who deserve it. What of the others? Those brave students who accompany their parents to an evening where they know their misdeeds will be raked over publicly can at least be congratulated for turning up.

I look up to see the Palmers moving towards my desk. Their son Callum is a wonder, producing perfect copper–plate maths every time. Mr Palmer takes a seat after shaking my hand: he looks successful, thrusting, business–like. Mrs Palmer sits beside him, bright and vivacious, with bullet–proof social skills. They have that pushy, upper-middle–class feel.

'Callum, why don't you take a seat from over there?' I suggest. For all his brilliance, he's a diffident lad. He looks towards a free chair.

'No, that's okay, he can perch on my shoulder,' says Mrs Palmer. 'Can't you, love?'

Callum looks awkward in his tightly–belted coat as he leans unhappily against his mother. This isn't the seating arrangement that I'd choose, but I decide to plough on.

'Where to start?' I say gamely, smiling at Callum and then at his parents. I trot out superlatives, and the parents nod; they've heard it all many times before, it's simply a question of whether I can outdo the legions of teachers who have lauded Callum's work in the past. They watch me intently, and I falter; just as in the classroom, it's easy to talk too much on these occasions.

'How do you see things?' I ask hopefully. 'Does Callum talk much about his maths at home?'

Mr and Mrs Palmer pause and exchange a glance. Callum shifts his weight from one foot to the other.

'Callum enjoys his maths,' says Mr Palmer, 'but we wonder sometimes, is he being stretched?'

I recall that I have a bulging briefcase full of scripts to mark. I think to myself, 'Callum may not be being stretched, but I am.'

'There's always extension material available,' I say calmly, and semi–truthfully. 'There's the extra–curricular group on Tuesday lunchtimes that Callum comes along to. And Callum is wonderful when it comes to teaching his peers. If you can teach a fellow–student, you can be sure you understand the material. Isn't that right, Callum?'

Callum nods. He senses that he's caught in adult cross–fire.

'What do you plan to do with your life, Callum?' I add, 'because if you go into maths you'll be snapped up.'

'What careers can you go into with maths?' asks Mr Palmer, 'beyond being a maths teacher, of course.'

'Of course, what kind of loser goes into maths teaching?'

This is the reply I briefly consider before deciding that my career is worth holding on to.

'There's a marvellous website I can recommend,' I say. 'I'll give you the address tomorrow, Callum.'

'We'd like to look at that together,' says Mrs Palmer, 'the three of us. Wouldn't we, Callum?'

I muffle a sigh, and take another sip of coffee. What am I hearing?

Callum is our creation. We have no intention of allowing him to choose by himself.

Why can't Callum's folks just look amazed at how well he is doing, say 'Blimey!' and add, 'Where does he get it from? Search us. Thank you.'

At last I find some courage from somewhere.

'Sure, but it's your life, Callum,' I say, looking him straight in the eye. 'Don't you agree, Mr and Mrs Palmer?'

Li Yang

There was one lad in Tower Hamlets whose character I found especially admirable, a quiet, hard-working child of Chinese heritage called Li Yang. He was eleven, bright, extremely so, and sensitive too - the noise in my classroom got to him even more than it got to me. This school was not a place for such pupils, or indeed, such staff.

One day, he came up at the end of a lesson.

'I'd like to give you this, Sir,' he said quietly.

It was a poem. It was beautifully expressed, and talked of his feelings about life in that school. His dignified pain and unhappiness was evident in every line. He was a remarkable child, old before his time.

Li was on my side as I tackled rowdy classes, but as the year progressed, I could sense even his support for me ebbing away. My presence in front of such a group was becoming more questionable. On one particularly bad day, he cracked.

'Just think how much work I'd be doing if I was in Mrs Davison's class!' he said out loud, looking straight at me.

My last buttress in the group had gone, the last person flying a flag for me had withdrawn their support. Could I really turn this around now?

Non-Mathematicians

Maths A Levels are at the moment unique, in that you can choose to do two of them. On offer are Maths and Further Maths (if you're super-keen you can do Additional Further Maths as well). I'm today teaching a Year Two group at A Level, and the way the timetabling has fallen, half of my students are doing Maths A Level, while the other half are taking both Maths and Further Maths.

There's a question on the board I know the Further Maths clientele will find easy (we've already covered this in Further), so I try to leave them out of the group to answer this.

'This is for the non-Further Mathematicians only,' is what I mean to say.

What I actually say is, 'This is for the non-mathematicians only.'

Students are extraordinarily slow to drop a mistake like this. For the rest of the year, the single maths cohort refer to themselves as the non-mathematicians with a clear sense of grievance.

'Is this for the mathematicians? Or the non-mathematicians, Jonny?'

'Getting us non-mathematicians through A Level, Jonny, must be a nightmare.'

'I think, Jonny, you're going to need a mathematician for that one.'

Each time, I'm reduced to gibbering apologies, but forgiveness is painfully withheld.

'Would it help if I refer to myself as a non-teacher?'

Gardening

It's summer, and it's the holidays. Any teacher who denies that this perk of our job is indeed a mighty blessing is lying. After arising at a modest hour of the day, I emerge from our kitchen to spend a little time in our garden. Living in a mid–terrace house in Norwich as we do, this is thin, but surprisingly long. It divides into two patio areas separated by a handkerchief of lawn, with long beds either side. If I count the plants, we have perhaps twenty–five major shrubs, which reminds me – of a classroom of twenty–five students. As I potter amongst the weeds, I reflect on the parallels between gardening and teaching.

Plants are different, and students are different. Some plants survive whatever; you are guaranteed a healthy crop of flowers even if you ignore them completely. I can think of many robust ex–students who would have achieved great things had I given them a textbook and nothing else. Other living creatures are more sensitive, requiring prolonged attention and tenderness. Can we find a more productive place for this plant in this garden? (Have you got your seating plan right?) Would full sun (sitting at the front table) or partial shade (towards the back of the class on the left) be beneficial? I find it a joy to dig up and move a struggling plant and watch it recover. (This is akin to retaining a student who initially says he wants to leave, but who in the end is glad he's stayed the course.)

Not every plant flowers at the same time of year (and thanks be for that). That's also true of students' mathematics careers. Some underachieve at GCSE, for any of a multitude of reasons, then flourish at A Level, while others peak at GCSE and find A Level harder. Others achieve modestly at A Level, but then choose to further their maths at the right university, and a PhD can follow.

A garden can be taken over by pests, as a classroom can be invaded, perhaps, by a sense of ennui. Are you as a teacher or gardener going to react in an organic way (point out the problem to the class in a calm and restorative fashion), or are you going to give them a blast of chemicals (read the riot act)?

But there are differences between gardens and classrooms. We choose our plants, at least the new ones, but not our students. Students move on, hopefully without dying, while plants don't. We can put our plants into pots, and then, like students, they can be regrouped time and time again – but plants that have taken root in full soil can't be repositioned quite so easily.

I see my gardening as essentially a simple activity. Plants need water, feeding, pruning, the right amount of sunlight, the right soil and a certain amount of pest control. When do we need to prune a student? Might they be the one who has their hand up first for every question? The sunlight needs to be shared. If I get these basics right, the vast majority of plants will flourish. Then I can reach for the gardening theory books for that remaining fraction.

A garden sleeps over winter, before growing to a great display of energy and activity in the summer months. Likewise, the classroom is dormant over the summer holidays, but crescendos to a cacophony of effort and striving come the exams that come ever closer to Spring. Maybe we DO try to get our plants to all flower together (it's easy to misspell 'gardener' as 'gradener'…).

Letting Down the Sisterhood

The Englishman Arthur Cayley and the Irishman William Rowan Hamilton are jointly credited with discovering the Cayley-Hamilton theorem, which says that any square matrix (square array of numbers) satisfies its own characteristic equation (so $A = \begin{pmatrix} 1 & 2 \\ 3 & 4 \end{pmatrix}$ has the characteristic equation $\lambda^2 - 5\lambda - 2 = 0$, and it is true that $A^2 - 5A - 2I = 0$). I remember showing this to the Further Maths group one day, only for Sally to let out a sigh as I concluded by explaining the history of the result.

'I was really, really wishing that the Cayley–Hamilton Theorem was proved by a thirteen–year–old girl called Kayleigh Hamilton,' she said, disappointed.

As with so many parts of life, women have a steep hill to climb when it comes to maths. The history of the subject does contain some acknowledged female voices, but they're usually drowned out by a man brandishing his theorem in his right hand while holding a mug of hot tea and a homemade biscuit in his left, both presumably supplied by some unthanked woman in the background.

We try our damnedest at my college to provide a level playing field, and in certain areas of our subject, we succeed in recruiting an equal gender balance, which is at least a start. But still in mechanics, the applied branch of mathematics to do with motion and forces and centres of gravity, girls are heavily outnumbered by boys.

But just occasionally, a girl fails to help the cause. Katy is one of only two female students in my Mechanics group, and I'm trying to encourage her.

Me: So Katy, what are you going to do with your life?

Katy: I'd like to get into Formula One.

Me: What, designing engines?

Katy: No, I'd like to marry a racing driver.

This Hurts Me More

I spent plenty of time in St Philip Howard struggling to put together a humane philosophy of punishment. Clearly if a student's been unreasonable (and that applied to plenty of shennanigans in my lessons), there had to be consequences, or else as night follows day, there would be a repeat. What should those consequences look like? I had to find something students didn't like, without being gratuitously vindictive. What my youngsters really didn't like was, in fact, fairly constant; they hated having their spare time wasted. An ex-headmistress I visited for mentoring laughed as I told her of my travails.

'The real punishment for a youngster is to be made to keep completely still! I used to ask kids to just lie flat on a table for fifteen minutes; after five, they would be pleading to be allowed down!'

I should say her students were younger than mine; my head-mistress friend had taught at primary level. I was, however, in the mood to try anything once. Next detention I said, 'Now Gary, I want you to lie down on this table, please.'

He looked at me suspiciously.

'Are you kinky, then, Sir?'

How about setting lines? Old-school, but certainly, kids hated these. Brian, my senior tutor, was strongly anti-lines, which he saw as totally worthless. But then, he argued that setting mathematics as a punishment couldn't be right either; lesson work should be a pleasure, and setting it as a punishment was contradictory.

'Bring in some encyclopaedias,' he said airily, after I'd picked his brains over detentions for the nth time. 'At least they'll come out of it with a few research skills.'

The next day, I struggled in with the twelve battered volumes of my Children's Britannia, the encyclopaedia I'd used as an eleven-year-old. I had a detention with Rich, Anthony and Clive, three serial miscreants, at the end of the day. Miraculously they all turned up. Still reeling with amazement, I posted three queries on the board, and pointed to the pile of books.

'I want the answers! You'll find them in there!'

The questions were:
Where was Atlantis?
Who's the leading goal-scorer for England?
Who was Karl Jung?

The three boys took one look at the board, and within five seconds they'd answered one question each without touching the red tomes I'd heaved so laboriously into work.

'Atlantis is in Hackney,' said Rich.

'Harold Wilson scored a load of goals for England,' offered Anthony.

'And Karl Jung is your uncle!' concluded Clive.

They looked at each other, said a communal, 'That's it!', and disappeared, running away down the corridor.

205

Reconstruction

Some years ago, builders arrived at our home to create a loft conversion. The experience was traumatic, as every room in the house filled with small bits of rubble, but the end result was a delight.

'Maybe I'm in the same business,' I thought, 'helping my students to extend their mental homes.'

What would a good mathematical extra room look like? Strong but flexible, it would have considered all the pitfalls, and it'd be properly linked to the rest of the house. Of course, a loft conversion that failed to meet these criteria might need rebuilding.

Lucy, the daughter of friends, was battling anorexia. No longer in school, she was in need of a maths tutor, and I was glad to help. Full of anxieties, some completely irrational, it was not a surprise to find she viewed her mathematics fearfully. This is what happened when we started work on fractions.

'Start with an open question,' I told myself. 'Lucy, can you give me two fractions that add to 2/3?'

1/3 + 1/3. 'Fine. And another pair?'

3/9 + 2/6. 'And another?'

4/12 + 5/15.

'No problems with equivalent fractions,' I thought, relieved. 'Now, can you give me two differently–sized fractions that add to 2/3?'

Lucy thought, then wrote 3/9 + 3/9, then crossed out the top 3 and replaced it with a 4, then crossed out the second 3 and replaced it with a 2.

4/9 + 2/9.

'Pretty smart,' I thought. 'Have I underestimated Lucy?' A flash of nervousness crossed my mind.

Then she said, 'But doesn't 4/9 + 2/9 add to 6/18?' A misconception! My mental calm returned. We talked this through, before I asked, 'Can you give me two fractions that <u>multiply</u> to 2/3?'

Lucy wrote $\dfrac{2}{3} = \dfrac{8}{12} = \dfrac{2 \times 4}{4 \times 3} = \dfrac{2}{4} \times \dfrac{4}{3}$. Pretty smart again.

'So with multiplication, we multiply the tops, and multiply the bottoms: but do you know how to <u>divide</u> one fraction by another?'

'No, I don't,' she said. I reached into my fractions toolkit, and dispensed the never–before–challenged line, 'Turn the second one upside down, and replace the divide with a times.'

We experimented with this, before Lucy asked, 'So with dividing fractions, can you divide the tops and divide the bottoms?'

My own fractions loft conversion suddenly experienced a painful jolt, as if someone had applied a swift blow with a sledgehammer. I watched it totter, before it finally came to rest at an unacceptable angle to the horizontal. Throughout my school career, my university study, and my long time in teaching, I had never entertained such a thought. And a few moments later, we saw that her intuition was precisely correct.

$$\frac{\left(\dfrac{8}{9}\right)}{\left(\dfrac{4}{3}\right)} = \frac{2}{3}.$$

But her demolition of my fractions extension had only just begun.

'So does the same apply to subtracting fractions then?' she asked innocently. 'Can you turn the second fraction upside down and replace the minus with a plus?'

I could see a large metal ball on the end of a crane swinging towards my fractional roof. I had not the faintest idea.

1/3 – 1/5 = 1/3 + 5/1. No chance. So could this rule <u>ever</u> be true? I did a feverish calculation on a bit of scrap, as much for my sanity as anything else.

$$\frac{a}{b} - \frac{c}{d} = \frac{a}{b} + \frac{d}{c} \Leftrightarrow c^2 = -d^2.$$

So this equation only possibly had answers within complex numbers.

Feeling a fraud, I set Lucy some questions to work on at home. I surveyed the wreckage I would be repairing as my own homework. Perhaps the fractions structure I'd eventually arrive at would be less rigid than the old one when faced with surprises.

'See you,' said Lucy with a polite smile as she left.

'See you,' I said weakly. What might next week's topic be?

Tom

Tom looks at me resentfully. 'Sorry, Jonny,' he says. My anger dissipates.

I'm holding his mechanics assignment, handed in late, one of three he owes me. It's a swiftly–executed copy of the specimen answers, presumably borrowed from someone else. A few numbers and expressions have been altered to give the impression of authenticity, but I've not been fooled. At least he's admitted the crime.

'What about Cambridge, Tom?' I ask. Tom is (usually) one of the brightest students I've ever taught. He wants to go to Cambridge, and he ticks my criteria for this; lightning assimilation of concepts and techniques, with a creative mind and a healthy (sometimes too healthy) self–confidence. The only question–mark is a wildness of temperament, leading to unreliability.

'If I get there, I get there,' says Tom defiantly, 'or somewhere else.'

'What if that somewhere else doesn't stretch you?' I ask.

Tom shakes his head. 'Oh, I'll get to Cambridge. I'll work at the end, like I did last year.'

Tom's mercurial approach caused a scare at AS, but he shut himself away to revise for a solid fortnight, with spectacular results. He has an offer from Cambridge that is achievable. But in his A2 year, girlfriends have taken over.

'A2 is different to AS, Tom,' I say, truthfully. 'It's much harder to be last minute. This is February. If you dedicate yourself to study from now till July, you CAN do it.'

Tom works in a local bar. 'How many hours paid work are you doing?' I ask gently. 'Fifteen a week? Twenty a week?'

Tom says nothing. I sigh.

'Twenty–five a week. Can't you see how crazy that is, Tom? What would going to Cambridge do for your earning power over a career? You do the math.'

'I need the money,' he says stubbornly.

'For your social life?' I ask. 'Can't you put that on ice temporarily? Unless – you need the money for other reasons?'

Tom's eyes say, 'Don't go there.' Some of our students support their families. I change tack.

'The thing is, Tom, I just don't think you're taking my exam results seriously enough,' I say.

Our eyes meet, and we manage a brief smile, before I sigh again.

'I can't stand over you with a big stick, nor can your parents. Even if we did, who'd do that for you at Cambridge? At your first job? It has to come from you.'

'It's just that I don't like being told what to do,' says Tom gruffly. 'Are we done?'

I look at this boy–man with sadness, as he stands and heads for the door. 'Tom', I say quietly. 'I'm only asking, do yourself justice.'

Tom gives me one last stare, before turning and closing the door behind him.

Tom carrying on working in his bar, and consuming its products. He missed most lessons that were first thing in the morning, which included all of mine. He moved from handing in copies of assignment answers to handing in nothing. I did all I could in terms of liaising with his tutor and his parents, but by now it was too near to the exams to do much. To withdraw him would have been cruel. On Results Day, I found him sobbing behind a bush – he'd failed four out of six of his Year Two maths modules. He'd been given a B for Maths, based largely on his Year One results, and an E for Further Maths. I did my best to console him. A year later, he asked the college for a reference, naming all of his old teachers as referees, except for me.

Authority

My problems with teaching in Tower Hamlets did not go unnoticed. Was I avoiding the staffroom? Looking back, concerned colleagues kept me on their radar more than I realised. That included Paula, my Head.

One day she came into my classroom to talk to my form. The silence they granted her was palpable. As they left, she stayed for a motherly chat, her smile heart-warming in the morning sunshine.

'That authority you have, Paula,' I asked brazenly, 'where does it come from?'

'It comes from your subject,' she said, thoughtfully, 'which for me was Geography. In my first year as a teacher, I suffered like you. But eventually I saw that I wanted the kids to behave because I felt so awful when they didn't. Gradually I moved instead towards wanting the kids to behave because if they didn't, Geography wasn't learnt, and that was the only reason, really, that we were together at all.'

I nodded.

'Your authority comes from your subject,' said Paula, repeating herself like any good teacher. 'Together with the intensity with which you want your students to learn it.'

She got up, and headed for the door, before turning again.

'Oh, and yes, the odd bit of technique helps too.' She grinned. 'You'll get there, Jonny.' She put on another large smile, one that looked forced this time, and closed the door.

Sex and Maths

I'm writing something about functions on the board when I hear whispers on the table behind me.

'Are you still going out with Danny? No, we split up, didn't you know? Why? He cheated on me! No!'

It's pointless to get uptight at this point. You have to take the conversation and work with it. With a sigh, I try this;

'Let me tell about a friend of mine, who went out with a function he thought was nice and even,

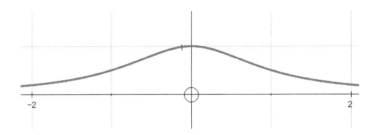

until it turned out she was a bit odd:

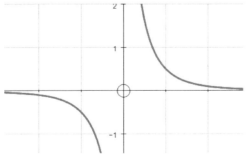

213

so now he's with a periodic function, and yes, they've had their ups and downs…'

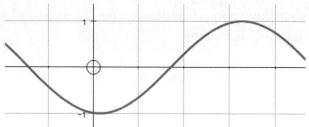

I'm not claiming that this is stand-up comedy of the highest order, but it's a better response than throwing angry warnings about. Students appreciate that you are trying to improvise within their world for a moment, and they're grateful for that.

The completely sex–free maths lesson does not exist. Taking sketching a quartic, for example. A quartic curve is one involving powers of x where the highest power is 4, for example, $y = x^4 -3x^3 + x - 1$, which gives

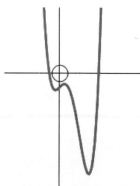

Innocent enough, but $y = 4x^4 - 2x^2$ looks like this.

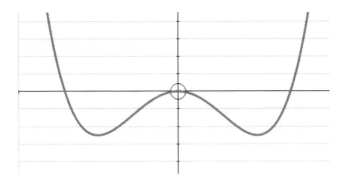

Every maths teacher will have lost count of the number of times they've had to cry, 'They're just turning points on a graph, I tell you!'

The research literature poignantly quotes the example of a student struggling to get out the word 'infinity', but who instead says 'infidelity' every time. What's happened in his family?

All that said, I often find the way students get distracted in their maths lessons by talking about their recent sexual conquests (or lack of them) something of a bore. So I was interested one day to observe my colleague Julian teach an English lesson on *Tis A Pity She's A Whore*. Management liked us to watch practitioners from subjects other than our own, and Julian was regarded as one of the star performers at Paston. He and his class didn't disappoint.

I confess, I'd not read the play, but it immediately becomes clear that sex here, far from being an annoying diversion, is the essential subject matter.

'I'd like you to come up with five different seduction strategies used in this passage,' says Julian busily.

Why chat off the subject when the subject matter of the lesson itself is so chat–worthy? '*Are you still going out with Danny?*' Exactly the discussion required for the analysis of this text. There are nodding faces amongst the students. Their lives, indeed, the most precious bits of their lives, are providing the raw material for this lesson.

They report back. 'His first strategy was to lie to her.'

Can lying really be a seduction technique? Young people relate to the idea of lying. Unless they are extraordinarily virtuous, they'll be experimenting with telling untruths themselves. To be able to explore this in the context of their learning, within a classroom, is exciting; an invitation to taste forbidden fruit.

Afterwards, I muse to myself, as I walk back across the broad lawns that lie between the English classrooms and the mathematics ones.

'Can maths lessons really be like this? Pythagoras's Theorem is hopefully a truth and not a lie. But surely we can aim for an easy conversation that does not exclude gentle laughter at diagrams that come out wrong. And the lives of the mathematicians often contain plenty of drama that can helpfully break up a lesson with human levity.'

Climbing the stairs, I reach my classroom, and have a few moments to gaze out at the flowers rambling in our college beds. I feel blessed to have such a view.

'Maths does not have to be forbiddingly pure,' I decide. 'And if we maths teachers make it earthier, then maybe our students wouldn't feel the need to discuss chaps like Danny quite so much?'

Looking Sheepish

There's a story I love, about a hapless maths teacher who enters his classroom and starts on his first problem by saying, 'Let x be the number of sheep.'

A brave student in the back row puts his hand up.

'Suppose it's not?'

As the story goes on, the philosopher Wittgenstein was asked if the student's remark was trivial.

He thought hard for three days, and eventually said, 'No, it's not.'

McMathematics

I was asking Laura about shapes one day.

'So you've drawn a pentagon, Laura, that's good, but the question talks about it being a regular pentagon. Do you know what the word regular means here?'

She looked beseechingly up at me.

'Medium-sized?'

The Mark of a Good Teacher

What will education be like in the Kingdom of Heaven? Might there be less marking? Students will get feedback, of course, in that blessed land, but more directly from their teacher in lessons. There'll be self–assessment, and peer–marking, and what's more, our little darlings will actually carry this out, religiously.

What will the Kingdom of Heaven exclude? A weary teacher forcing themselves to get up at four in the morning to mark a scrappy set of answers before heading into a school day for which they are hideously under–prepared and ludicrously over–tired.

My marking regime sometimes felt like this:

1. Inform Mrs G that I am not to be disturbed for any reason whatsoever.
2. Head up to study and shut door.
3. Clear desk by forming large pile of just-paid bills, articles and junk mail, and place onto floor.
4. Place scripts to be marked in middle of now empty desk.
5. Search for red biro. Black and blue biros abound, but no red to be seen. Eventually find red biro underneath pile of just-paid bills.
6. Decide to mark to music. Opt for Mozart.
7. Look at pile of scripts. Breathe deeply.
8. Piece of Mozart is proving a distraction, since piece is too well–known. Switch to Beethoven.
9. Some of the homeworks are on paper ripped from spiral–bound notebooks, creating jagged edges that are a health hazard (paper

cuts can be nasty). Work through scripts, carefully cutting off dangerous borders.

10. Look at top script. Wonder how to model mathematically the time T it takes for me to mark a set of scripts.

11. 'How about $T = a + bn$, where n is number of scripts and where a and b are constants?' Start doing rough calculations on piece of scrap paper to determine a and b.

12. Beethoven string quartet is proving too emotive, and is thus as distracting as Mozart. Switch to Schubert symphony.

13. Breathe deeply again. How many scripts are there here? Count them. Lift scripts and knock them into more exact A4 shape, thus also aerating them in the process to make them more markable.

14. Put red biro to paper with groan. Forget Golden Rule of Marking (start with your best student) and mark the script on the top of the pile (produced by worst student.) Award a score of 10% and feel depressed.

15. Schubert symphony is proving more emotive than Beethoven. Opt for silence.

16. Mrs G calls through the door that Chelsea–Liverpool game is on the box, there is 20 minutes left and score is 3–3. I shout that I am not to be disturbed for any reason and I will be down in 30 seconds.

I would, being honest, have to rate the above as a bad day at the office. Marking for me was, sometimes, a real pleasure – there were days I could cut through a pile of scripts like a chef dicing cucumber. I would visualise the person whose work I was addressing, I would wish them well with their maths even if they were a toe–rag last lesson, and I would challenge myself to comment as helpfully as I could in the time available.

219

Examiners do essential work, but how much harder must it be to mark the scripts of strangers? It was only being able to put the work to a face that made the job even the tiniest fun for me. But there, I've said it, the word 'fun' can be attached to the word 'marking'. So does the Kingdom of Heaven contain a hint of this after all?

Alan's Advice

I was half-way through the summer term at St Philip Howard, and things still hung precariously in the balance. The good weeks were enjoyably tantalising, but this was one of my down weeks, and I was on playground duty, which meant watching a few lads kick a tennis ball around a scuffed bit of tarmac. I surveyed the grim concrete slabs that made up the walls of this unforgiving school, and their greyness struck a chord.

Under a tree eating a packet of crisps was Alan, one of my tutor group, twelve years old yet infinitely more streetwise than I was. If I'd been forced to pigeonhole my students, then with no debate Alan would've been placed gently into the box labelled, 'Likeable Rogues.' I'd said to him once, whilst walking together down a corridor, 'Alan, I saw your folks at Parent's Evening last night.'

He didn't break step. 'Sorry about them, Sir,' he replied. 'Right pair of nutters.'

It was a mark of how desperate I was that I now walked over to tackle him. He looked up from his crisps, surprised.

'Alan,' I said, as he watched his footballing mates. 'Can I ask you something?'

Alan looked suspicious. 'Okay.' This was a long way from the safety of the classroom.

'Why is it, Alan, that you do everything that Mrs Davison tells you to do, but nothing that I tell you to do?'

I knew I was breaking the rules here. Teachers should not ask such a question. Alan looked into my eyes, clearly as puzzled as I felt. He scratched his nose, before giving his answer.

'It's just that Mrs Davison, Sir,' he said slowly, 'she - keeps the act up.'

He looked back up at me, then walked away. He really had been, genuinely, trying to help.

Favorito

Mrs G has battled with me to include this.

Mrs G: Ask me who my favourite Irish mathematician is.

Me: Who's your favourite Irish mathematician?

Mrs G: Fib O'Nacci.

Howlers

Vernon, a Paston student of mine, is giving us a talk on the great Italian mathematician Fibonacci. His presentation is poised, and he's scoring points heavily. As I listen, I idly wonder if Fibonnacci's master work *Liber Abaci*, the number theory tome published in 1267, will get a mention. I'm not disappointed.

'Fibonacci's most famous book,' says Vernon confidently, 'was called *Liberace*,' and he had a PowerPoint slide to back this up. I stare at the screen, puzzled. Liberace's career as a flamboyant pianist goes back a long way, I know, but was his first biography really published in the thirteenth century? My class are surprised when their teacher's shoulders start to shake.

When it comes to student howlers, I have an angel on one shoulder and a devil on the other. The angel looks solemn and says this;

'Isn't there something tyrannical about your laughing at your students' errors? We all make mistakes, and we don't like to have them ridiculed. If you're trying to promote a culture in your classroom where questions, any questions, are welcome, then to lampoon howlers is to say the least contradictory. If you enjoy it when your students are idiots, then might they not become idiots just to please you?'

I nod sheepishly, and feel guilty. But then the devil on the other shoulder has a word:

'My comrade's speech contains truth, but isn't it a little severe? Teaching, as you know, can sometimes feel like the perpetual triumph of hope over experience. It's disheartening to find that lessons that are

223

beautiful in your own eyes have not created understanding of comparable beauty within your students. Sometimes the gap between what you hope your students have learnt and what their answers show that they've learnt is so great that you must either laugh or cry. If their answers do contain a grain of humour, then accept that gratefully, as a way of lessening the pain.'

It's worth remembering that teachers too can commit a howler from time to time. Once, at the end of a long day, Louise asked me what λ stood for in the vector equation of a line, $\underline{r} = \underline{a} + \lambda\underline{b}$.

'Ah, yes, lambda is a constant that varies,' I said wearily.

Louise repeated this back to me slowly. 'Lambda is a constant that varies?'

After five minutes of delirious laughter, I amended this to 'a scalar that varies.' But I'll not be surprised if my students repeat that to each other at future reunions in local public houses; 'Do you remember the day Jonny told us about, "the constant that varies"?'

Mrs G's school is a good howler source. She reports a story told to her by her history colleague, who was attempting to discuss the Warsaw Ghetto with his pupils. At the end of the lesson, he fields this question; 'If a ghetto is such a bad thing, how come Santa has one?'

The best mistakes are those that create appealing alternative vistas in your mind, fresh perspectives that it'd be hard to arrive at any other way. Here are my three favourite howlers committed by my students, all of which do this.

Number one: a student working on their Numerical Methods coursework narrowly misses writing the word 'definitely' in their write-up of the Newton-Raphson Method.

This method defiantly misses the root.

I smile to picture Mister Newton and Mister Raphson shaking their fists at this elusive solution whilst shouting, 'We'll get you next time, wait and see!'

Secondly, I find this somehow touching.

'The distribution peeks at 7...'

This summons up for me the vision of a party where the attractive and flirtatious Miss Seven is being admired by Mister Normal, a shy man with an overly-symmetrical head on the other side of the room.

And finally, in a statistics lesson I once asked, 'A parameter of a distribution, now, if I used that phrase, what might I be thinking of?'

I was hoping to hear, 'The mean?' or 'How about "the variance"?' but instead I heard, 'Would you be thinking of the distance around the outside?'

Avalanche

A while ago I chanced across the cracking word 'lubbing', short for 'looking up in the back of the book.' In a maths classroom, this activity certainly deserves a name. 'Lubbing' carries connotations of 'lubrication', which judicious use of the answers can certainly provide. There's also a hint of 'land-lubber', someone too cautious, maybe, to set out on their own mathematical ocean unaccompanied.

Every mathematics teacher is an educational researcher of some kind, whether they realise it or not, and the literature of mathematics education encourages classroom practitioners to become namers. New words suggest 'extended metaphors', that become 'gathering points' for discussion, 'resonant labels' that we can share with others. These are new wordinesses to describe new words that describe things that are hopefully worth noticing.

One day in the classroom, a phenomenon so tiny as to be ruled negligible by many grasped my attention, and I tried to find a name for it. The event was this: a student would call me over, and I'd spot a key weakness in their argument. Often it needed no word from me (preferably it needed no word from me), just a friendly finger. Then followed the 'Aaahh!'

It was the quality of that 'Aaahh!' that interested me. It could be short or drawn out, loud or soft, pleased or annoyed, proud or ashamed. Everybody's 'Aaahh!' was different, but it always meant, 'I see now.' Occasionally there was an more or less implicit 'Thank you!' tacked on the end, but that was rare.

Can the 'Aaahh!' be faked? In a maths classroom, most of the time, I believe the 'Aaahh!'s are genuine (although an 'Aaahh!' could be premature – 'Aaahh! I see - er – no, I don't…')

How should the teacher respond to the 'Aaahh!'? Should I stay and help in the ensuing reconstruction? I always headed off swiftly to the next raised arm, abandoning the student to rebuild for themselves from the rubble of their solution, alone or in the company of their colleagues.

My naming for the 'Aaahh!' event eventually settled on 'avalanche.' *An overwhelming influx*, my dictionary says. 'Avalanche' comes from 'avaler', Old French for 'to descend'. That fits - the student's solution has somehow 'got above itself'. 'Avalanche' can also be a verb; the teacher 'avalanches' the problem for the student, to produce that precious 'Aaahh!' I claim skillful avalanching is a good thing for a teacher to do.

What else does my dictionary tell me? 'An avalanche' is *a shower of particles produced after a high energy particle meets matter*. The results of an impact produced by something tiny, but extremely intense. Maybe the teacher who desires to avalanche must aim their 'particle' carefully; the greater the precision, the wider the shower produced.

I pause. Is my naming trite, even grandiose? Is the phenomenon it notices so quotidian as to be unworthy of the honour? As I gaze out of my empty classroom window at the College gardener mowing the grass and dandelion mix, I'm undecided. But one piece of naming could lead on to another.

'Who knows, if we noticed the everyday more and accorded it greater respect, we might reap surprising rewards,' I whisper. I turn to see a quotation from Albert Szent-Gyorgyi on my wall.

Discovery consists of seeing what everybody has seen,
and thinking what nobody has thought.

The Second Year

I often talked to my Tower Hamlets colleagues about their experience of becoming a teacher, and the message back was uniformly hopeful.

'You won't believe how much easier it all is in your second year.'

Margaret was adamant. 'Come back next year, Jonny, and the kids will have accepted you. They settle down in Year Two, believe me. We've all been through it.'

I was, slowly, learning techniques, that much I had to agree with. One day, I was called in by Paula.

'I'm recommending that you pass your probationary year, Jonny,' she said with her trademark broad smile. 'Welcome aboard the teaching profession!' I ran whooping into the staffroom. The four other probationary teachers that I'd started with were there dancing too; we'd all had similar news.

'Oh, yes, Sir, with the grade ones and twos!' said Susie, mimicking our pupils beautifully.

Three weeks later, I taught my final lesson of Year One. That evening, I threw industrial-sized boxes of paperwork out of cupboards for the caretakers to recycle. I looked around at my room, with its shiny brushed floor, with its colourfully postered walls, with its polished desks, ergonomically arranged, and I thought back to the bizarre maze I'd inflicted on the kids back in Lesson One. I'd learnt something.

'Year Two,' I sang out loud. 'Bring it on…'

Mathematician First

It's the Paston staffroom at break, and James, our biology teacher, has the floor. A barn owl couple with fledglings is currently nesting in his shed, and because strong young barn owls have a tendency to devour their weaker brethren, he was concerned. In an attempt to research this phenomenon further and maybe find some advice, James had typed 'chicks eating chicks' into Google, only to be referred to web-pages offering information rather different to that sought.

The laughter dies down as the telephone rings, and I look around the staff-room. What a mixed bunch we are.

'It's for you, Simon,' says Rochelle, who answers the phone more often than she should. I brush away a pang of guilt as I take a sip of tea.

'Take Simon,' I say to Philip, my neighbour, as we watch our harassed-looking colleague take the phone. 'He arrived here ten years ago, and in that time he's taught, at various levels, English, Sociology, Business Studies, Geography, General Studies and Psychology.'

Philip, my fellow tea-drinker this break-time, is our physics teacher. Retirement looms, and for him that day cannot come soon enough.

'You forget that this year he's teaching Construction Health and Safety to the BTEC group,' he says. 'You've seen him in his hard hat on a Monday?'

'He is the time-tabler's dream,' I sigh, feeling another flash of conscience.

'You stick down the immovable objects, the people who can only teach one thing, and then Simon fills the gaps,' says Philip admiringly. 'He's educational grout.'

I wonder to myself, 'Is this a life I would want?'

'Simon's a teacher first, and the subject comes second,' I muse, as our hero continues with his call. 'He loves teaching, and he's damn good at it. He's a primary teacher in a sixth form college. But I couldn't do that.'

Philip smiles unkindly. 'Let's face it, Jonny, you can't be arsed to learn another subject. As it is, the material in the one you've got hardly changes from year to year.'

'I could teach music,' I counter. 'But…'

Philip's interested now. 'But…?'

'I can't play classical piano, you know, reading and that. Jazz only.'

'You could teach music technology,' said Philip. 'All the rage these days.'

I sigh. 'The kids are into music that I'm not into.'

'You must have to teach bits of maths you don't like?' asks Philip, incredulous.

'I can honestly say there's no bit of maths that I can't enjoy,' I reply slowly.

'You're weird, you are,' Philip replies. 'But then to me, maths on its own always seems like a subject for losers. Physics,' he says proudly, 'is maths with a reason.'

I ignore the jibe. 'I'm a mathematician first and a teacher second,' I persist. 'If I couldn't teach maths, I wouldn't want to be a teacher. I'd want to be a mathematician.'

Philip indicates towards the notice-board. 'So this job they're advertising; cross-college teaching methods adviser for the college – not your bag, I take it?'

'Smart teaching methods are fine, but in my case, only as they apply to teaching maths.'

Philip takes his final swig of tea and stands to go. 'Thank God this college has got more Simons than Jonnys,' he says, giving me a friendly glance. He chuckles as he heads for the door. 'Only kidding.'

Simon's off the phone, and turns to pick up a box of computer leads. He swears lightly to himself about something.

'What next, Simon, and where?' I ask.

'IT Key skills, and God knows,' he says, granting himself a mini-break to dab his forehead. 'How about you?'

I know what I have next. Indeed, I've been looking forward to it all week. I'll be introducing the Max-Box problem to my AS Pure group. Given a one metre square piece of metal, what's the open box with the largest volume you can make by cutting four equal squares from the corners and folding up?

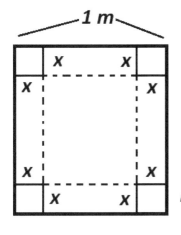

Choose x.
Throw away the four corners.
Fold along the dotted lines
to make a box.
For what value of x
is the volume a maximum?

This is an initiation into the usefulness of the differentiation part of the calculus. I've taught the lesson twenty times, and each time I love it more. I feel like a Jewish scribe creating a Torah scroll up at the board. Why is maths so indescribably beautiful? My kids worry about me sometimes.

I feel a third pang of guilt as I watch Simon replace his hanky and pick up his box.

'Oh, just maths, as always. In the usual room.'

233

Your Cheating Heart

I'm sitting in Robin's office together with Francis, a student of mine. I'm quaking with anger, which is rare for me. Robin is Head of Student Services at our college, and one of the nicest teachers you could wish to meet. He's just greeted Francis affably with a shake of the hand.

'How about a shake of the throat?' I think, for Francis has been caught cheating on his A Level Maths coursework.

Or has he? This much is true; he handed in a piece of coursework written by Mandy, a student who took the course last year. Francis had doctored the work by simply removing her name and inserting his. Francis might be considered unfortunate in a number of respects:

1. 'His' work was marked by me this year.
2. I was the teacher who marked Mandy's work last year.
3. I was in an alert mood, and
4. I still had Mandy's original filed away.

'What's the story, Francis?' asks Robin affably.

'Don't be nice to him, Robin!' my insides scream.

Francis, who looks suitably abject, comes up with this;

'I'm so sorry. I did toy with the idea that I might hand in Mandy's work as my own, but when it came to the crunch, I just, you know, couldn't do it. So I did the coursework myself, as I should have done all along. But then,' (Francis looks skywards) 'on the day of the deadline, I handed the wrong coursework in!'

He looks at the two of us, shrugs and smiles inanely, as if to say, 'What am I like?'

'Francis,' I ask, still furious, 'did any money change hands between you and Mandy over this?'

His mouth drops open, as though I've just asked him how he spent the fee he got for his grandmother. I spit bile for the rest of the meeting, while Robin thankfully lives out his commitment to creating a more peaceful world in impressive fashion.

It's now break–time, and I head upstairs to the staffroom. Over a mug of tea, I tell the story to my colleagues, and they too look shocked.

'You mean – this is a Year Two student?' asks Julian, horror-struck. 'He's been with us for eighteen months and he can't cheat better than that?'

If I was expecting sympathy, I was disappointed. The (light–hearted) consensus was that I had done a lamentable job in preparing Francis for this vital real–life skill.

Thinking back now, I sigh. Are we all not cheats? Aren't little half–lies part of even the most virtuous teacher's life? Francis's porkie pie, granted, was a big one; he could've been banned from all his A Level exams, creating a dent in his CV that would have taken years to remove. Yet if I'm honest with myself about my own impure actions, who am I to point the finger?

About a year ago, I went to a local meeting of A Level teachers focussing on a particular set of brand-new mathematics resources. Harry, a Head of Maths at a rival sixth form college, was vocal in his criticism.

'They're simply one matching activity after another,' he said. 'There's nothing ground-breaking here.'

'I think they're better than that, Harry!' I said hotly.

These activities had, in fact, been written by a friend of mine, and I defended her spiritedly. Harry caught me with a piercing eye; he'd clearly detected inauthenticity in my voice.

'Let's discuss one of these A Level tasks that you, Jonny, have actually used in your classroom, shall we?' he suggested.

I found myself in a spin. I'd used the GCSE versions in my lessons, and I'd explored some of the A Level ones at conference, but had I actually used one of these activities within my own A Level lessons? I realised to my shock, as all eyes in the room were on me, that I'd not.

'Er – okay – how about the one you mentioned earlier?' I replied lamely.

Harry looked triumphant. He'd made me dissemble; I'd claimed to teach a lesson that I'd not taught. The rest unrolled gradually; a conversation with my managers at College led to steady pressure until I wrote the required letter of apology. That particular piece of humble pie proved less than tasty.

So Francis, perhaps I was wrong to be so angry that day, and maybe Robin was right to treat your misdemeanours with gentleness. I'll take the beam out of my own eye before helping you with the mote in yours; and when it comes to cheating, let he who has never cheated cast the first stone.

Cracking Lesson

'Hi, folks!' It was September, Year Two was beginning, and I greeted my colleagues with an uncomplicated positivity. Yes, I arrived back in Tower Hamlets after the long summer break with a sizeable spring in my step. At last, the promise of studious customers and the chance to crack on with some serious mathematics. That was the script, but as I swiftly discovered, no one seemed to have given my students a copy.

Year Two was not only no better than Year One, but unfathomably worse. Year One at least contained weeks of hope, where I walked the corridors feeling in the zone. Year Two became a long harsh descent into depression, while my students got louder and wilder.

Where was that quiet acceptance and willingness to get on with work that the old hands had anticipated? I faced my colleagues with my unhappiness, and they replied by shifting uncomfortably in the staffroom.

'I wonder what it is, then?' said Deborah, confused.

I'd laughed at Mr Lanchester, but the arrival of a new maths teacher who would laugh in turn at my story grew closer by the day. Why, why, why was I carrying on? Surely just get signed off ill, resign quietly, and put it all down to experience. Instead I was grimly aiming to see out the academic year and try somewhere new in September. My mind, body and spirit, however, had other ideas.

Looking back, there were all sorts of unresolved contradictions working through my psyche at the time; it wasn't just work that was the problem. I'd chosen a room in a house with friends that was complete psychological foolishness. I began to sleepwalk. An outer life of chaos was coming together with an inner life of confusion to create a storm that truly deserved the adjective 'perfect'.

Prompted by those around me, I started to see a counsellor called Henrietta, a last throw of the dice, and I was fortunate to pick someone both well-qualified and sympathetic. She tuned into my depression straight away.

'You're trying to recreate *To Sir with Love*,' she sighed. 'Well, it's a wonderful dream.'

I must have established a safe haven there. A few weeks later, in January 1987, my soul rose up against my conscious mind's rigid commands. Four months of profound depression was released in three days and nights of mania, where I slept not a wink. That Friday, the 13th, I taught bizarre lessons, as if in a trance. As I looked around my classroom, everything took on a gender, and curiously, the genders seemed to alternate. The floor was female, the table was male, the book was female, the pencil was male…

'That's PhD stuff,' warned Henrietta when I told her this later.

Did the pupils behave strangely too? Most, I think, were unaware of my exalted state, but Li Yang knew things were different that day. He looked at me shrewdly, and said, 'I don't like this.'

I travelled home before setting off for a weekend with friends in Cheshire. There my psychosis well and truly took hold. While alone in the house, as my friends took an afternoon walk across the moorland, I 'baptised myself' in the bath before responding to an imagined invitation to 'step over into the Kingdom of Heaven'. My friends arrived back to find me curled up in a ball. They called an ambulance that took me to hospital that Sunday. That Monday at St Philip Howard was the first day I'd missed since starting.

You Must Remember This

Today I re–introduce the idea of coordinates to my AS group. How to remember that (2, 3) means two across, three up, rather than the other way around? I reach into my own mathematical childhood and recall the phrase which echoes across the years still.

'You go IN the house, then UP the stairs.' Daniel immediately sticks his hand up with a glint in his eye. 'What if you're a burglar?'

He makes me reflect that one's person's aide–memoire is another person's mental stumbling block. When I consulted the English teacher Mrs G over this, she too challenged the idea of remembering A via remembering B.

'Why do we have to tell our students that *Necessary is coffee with two sugars*? Why not cut out the middle–man and just remember how to spell "necessary"!' she said.

Mrs G is always right, as I've learned painfully down the years. But could there be times when a friendly crutch for useful facts might be welcome? As educators we would prefer memory to be based on understanding, but where that's tough to achieve, might a harmless piece of mind-jogging equipment be allowed to come to our rescue?

I remember my first mnemonic (it's Mnemosyne, the Greek goddess of memory, who gives us the word). Aged eleven, I recalled that < stood for 'less than' by telling myself that < looked quite like a squashed L. Later I twigged that < had a small left hand end, and a big right hand end, so the notion that the symbol was trying to convey was actually embedded into the mark itself. This meant that no jog to the memory was necessary; the symbol was its own mnemonic, and it thus became in my eyes an inspired choice.

241

As our mathematical career progresses, certain things become second nature (nothing was ALWAYS second nature to us). My way of remembering < evolved as I used it more in increasingly sophisticated situations, yet even now at times of panic and stress, I catch myself regressing to my childhood idea of a squashed L.

Inventing mnemonics can be fun. I ran a mini–competition each year that went like this:

In statistics, what does 'negative skew' mean? It means that the hump of the distribution is to the right, and the tail is to the left. Positive skew means that that the hump is to the left and the tail is to the right. Can you come up with a mnemonic for this?

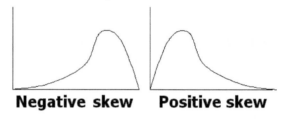

Negative skew   Positive skew

Claire one year suggested 'positive' and 'port' (= left) shared the same two starting letters. Angus offered that the second letter of 'plus' is 'l' for 'left'. But then, if you misremember these as 'a positively–skewed distribution has a TAIL to the left,' you're in trouble.

Jamie offered this improvement – imagine a p on its side, bubble up, and a g on its side, bubble up. Yes!

ᑫ pos neg ഇ

The Result Game

There were always two games going on in my classroom. One was the thrilling mental chess that was mathematics itself, and the second was the game of delivering good exam results. Most of the time these games ran along more or less happily side by side, but contradictions could arise, when the two perspectives banged violently into each other, resulting in waves of upheaval. There would be days, for example, when I longed to give my students more time on an activity, but that remorseless taskmaster the Scheme of Work would be sitting in the corner with its ready whip, directing me to wrap up these wonderful discussions and crack on with some exposition.

Teachers can be tempted to concentrate on one game and ditch the other. Two decades ago there was a maths teacher in one of our feeder schools who devoted every lesson exclusively to exploration, investigation and discussion. He was much loved, but his exam results were terrible. I'm not sure he would get away with that now, however admirable his ideals.

But then going the other way, concentrating on the exam to the exclusion of everything else, seems truly dismal. The class ends up drilled, with a brittle understanding that disappears the day after the exam. 'Please remember why you became a maths teacher in the first place,' I beg. But if your salary depends on exam results and those results alone, you can see why people sell out.

I would say the good maths teacher has to play both games, although the tension between the two can be hard to bear sometimes. So how did I do? How well did I teach the true maths game in all its glory to my students, and how well did we together play the more mundane exam game? The first question you will have to pose to my alumni; there is no hard data. The answer to the second question is that my, our, scores were mixed.

Every year our results arrived mid-August, with cheers and tears, but the real accounting came a few weeks later when the value-added data made its entrance. Raw results are fairly meaningless; if you go by those alone, then the teachers who teach the stronger classes will always do better. You need to consider the average GCSE score with which a student arrived, and see how they have performed at A Level against students nationally with a similar average GCSE score.

Using this statistical methodology for each course, our value-added system crunched maybe 200 hours of lesson time, a huge amount of mathematical blood, sweat and tears, into a single digit between 1 and 9. A score of 1 represented the best outcome in the country, while 9 represented the worst. The system allowed for more nuance than that; you could score a good 5, or scrape a 3. We in the maths department taught five courses in total, giving us five numbers each year.

I think I've been away from Paston long enough to say what happened; there's a new team in place now, who've probably cracked the value-added business. Suffice it to say that our scores averaged out over the years at below average.

That was the whole department score. How did I score compared with my colleagues? That doesn't seem like a particularly collegiate question to ask, but then one year I was hammered by management for having results that were marginally worse than my Head of Department, which wasn't very collegiate either. I would like to note that I only got hammered once.

244

Let's be generous and say I on average scored a 5 on my courses. Average for the country. Disappointing? Given my experience and qualifications, given that I was part-time and so had extra energy for the job, given my membership of improving organisations, and let's say it, given that Mrs G and I have no children, and thus inevitably have more time to devote to our jobs, then yes, disappointing.

My scores varied wildly. I regularly picked up a 2 for my Statistics 1 course, I have no idea why. But overall, the department was below average. We asked ourselves why each year. We were professionals, we cared, we knew our stuff, we'd been around the block, we'd taught at other schools and got good grades. We examined the value-added methodology and picked serious holes in it, but our non-mathematical managers nodded as their eyes glazed before haranguing us as if we'd said nothing.

Was it something in the water? Other Paston students in other subjects seemed to perform fine. I heard this idea voiced once; 'Is it that maths is just too abstract for Norfolk minds?' That seems more than a touch desperate, an unacceptably county-ist comment. The level of maths at the University of East Anglia provides a sound counterexample.

It's true we chose the MEI syllabus, generally regarded as the toughest. Could that be a factor?

I visited St Dominic's, the college in London where I'd taught before Paston, which regularly tops the league tables. 'How do you get these grades?' I asked pathetically. Roger, the Head of Department, smiled.

'We have a great many students from Indian and Chinese backgrounds. The level of parental ambition is stratospheric.'

Norfolk famously has a tiny ethnic minority population. I clutched this fact to my heart; was this the explanation?

In any school or college, one answer to getting good results is to become part of the lifeblood of the institution. You arrive, and no one knows anything about you. Gradually you engage with your colleagues, and if things go well, they begin to accept you. Little collaborations turn into professional loyalties, which turn into friendships. Subconsciously students realise that you are more and more part of the structure of the place, and you have communal firepower to call on. Your lessons improve, you give your students better work, so they do more and concentrate more. You have more energy, and positivity starts to snowball on all sides. Teaching is above all about the quality of the human relationships of which you are a part. As they grow, you move nearer to the heart of your workplace, and you find yourself increasingly loving it. There were years I felt like this, but at other times I felt excluded.

There were breaks in the clouds. An alternative measure of value added was trialled, and it made our department look better, because some attempt was made to compare like with like. And is 'average' so awful? Maths teachers the world over giggle at the headline,

Shock statistic; half of schools are below average.

But I still feel regretful about the grades we achieved. Could there be something further to consider? Was there some other factor in the background that was holding us back?

246

Collective

It's a whole staff meeting, and our leader is addressing us all.

'I was at a conference for sixth form college heads last week, and somebody there asked in their talk, "What's the collective noun for a group of principals?"'

She looked around the room, but no one had any idea.

'It's a "lack",' she said, pleased.

Her line was greeted with complete silence.

Interview Questions

'Mr Griffiths, it says here on your reference that you've had some problems with stress in the past. Would you like to talk about those?'

'Mr Griffiths, we'd like to ask you about your students' exam results in the last five years. How good have they been?'

'Mr Griffiths, your current principal happens to be a golf partner of mine…'

How did I prepare for a mathematics teaching interview? My CV was, of course, always truthful, but there are ways of saying truthful things that cover blemishes better than others. Any panel, however, was inevitably adept at spotting my euphemisms, those flaky bits of paintwork on the bodywork of my career that deserved a bit of a scratch with a 50p coin.

The same, of course, was true in reverse. While I was, if not hiding, then at least underplaying certain facts, then my prospective employers were guaranteed to be doing the same. The query, 'So how did this vacancy come to be advertised?' could often be enough to make sure the job was offered to someone else.

Let me tell you a story.

A sixth form college opens, and the Head of Maths is Mr A.

Mr A, a married man, begins an affair with a member of his department, Mrs B, a married woman.

Mr A's wife Mrs A learns of her husband's affair, and commits suicide.

How did Mrs A learn about Mr A's affair? Mr A accuses female members of staff of leaking the facts to her. He is persuaded to take early retirement. Mrs B teaches on.

Ms C is appointed as the new Head of Maths. She arrives from many miles away without selling her house first. This now starts to subside. She's forced to resign and return.

Mrs B is now given the Head of Maths job (options are limited), but then develops multiple sclerosis.

Mr D, the Second in Department, takes over from her as Head of Maths, but is given the job of Sector Leader as well, a workload that is completely unmanageable...

None of the above were me, but I certainly made my own contribution to this horror story.

The English department in our college rolled forward quietly with maybe two heads in twenty years, while others lurched from crisis to disaster to catastrophe, with a quick fix here and an emergency measure there. The mathematics department at Paston was described by Ralph, my Vice-Principal, as 'benighted' (we had seven Heads of Maths in the 23 years I was there).

I was frank about my history of illness at my interview for Paston (my referees certainly were). Would the interview panel have given me the job had they known absolutely everything there was to know about me? In that case, would anyone ever get any job? On the other hand, would I have taken the job had I known all the background? Maybe what the college needed was less of a mathematics teacher and more of an exorcist. In my time there, I wonder if I had a go at being both.

Take My Advice

I've reached the end of my classroom career. Maybe it's time to distil the wisdom that I've accumulated for the benefit of those maths teacher pups who come after me.

Never upset your caretaker.

Make sure your work on differentiation is well integrated, and that your work on integration is well differentiated.

Always laugh at your Principal's jokes.

When studying the equations of constant acceleration, do not claim that Suvat was the seventeeth century French mathematician who discovered them.

A mobile phone rings in your classroom. Before you haul the group over the coals, make sure that the phone is not yours.

Commit to memory the fact that $\cos(38°) = 0.78801$. Then when drawing a right–angled triangle, say carelessly, 'Let's make this angle, I don't know, 38°.' Then when you later need its cosine, appear to think hard with eyes closed before (slowly) writing down 0.78801... Enjoy the gasps of admiration as your work is checked, and watch your reputation spread.

If you feel the best way to tackle directed numbers is to draw a thermometer on the board, then fine, but try not to make it look like the male reproductive organ.

Try to work out who really runs your establishment. This is unlikely to be your Principal, and will probably be your caretaker.

When earnestly discussing with parents a worrying test score in your mark book, make sure it is not actually a book number.

If a student says, 'I am so sorry, I haven't done the homework, but I have a free next and I promise you will have it before lunchtime,' say 'At lunchtime I will swap your watch for your homework. Give your watch to me now.' If they don't have a watch, take their mobile phone. If they don't have a phone, then their shoes will do.

If challenged to compute $\cos 42^\circ$ in your head, laugh and say, 'Now that would be showboating!'

You may very occasionally be asked to cover a biology lesson. If you attempt to draw the male reproductive organ on the board, try not to make it look like a thermometer.

Be mightily aware that mobile phones can video anything that may happen in your classroom.

If your Principal asks to see you in his office, this may not be a joke. Especially if you've just been covering a biology lesson.

Set up a gospel choir singing songs that celebrate the good news that is mathematics. Call this choir *The Degrees of Freedom*.

When teaching a lesson on percentiles that is being observed by your Principal, do not try to calculate P_{45}.

Above all, remember that the secret behind all good teaching is integrity. Learn to fake this, and you'll be home and dry.

Recovery

I went back to teach in that East End school after my breakdown, but I knew within minutes that I had to leave. It was early 1989, and Tiananmen Square and the Berlin Wall could feel storms coming in their lives; I'd just experienced a true hurricane in mine, and I resigned without a job to go to. Margaret gave a sorrowful sigh when I told her; she'd invested a lot of time in me, and that, so it seemed, would not come to fruition now. Lofty had left Eastenders a year before; now it was my turn.

There were students I was greatly sad to say goodbye to. In our last lesson, Li gave me a present, a small rectangle wrapped in blue tissue paper. I opened it to find a Cub Scout Diary for 1989, which Alan grabbed from me and cruelly lampooned before the group. Its advice on *How to Untie Knots* would've been even more helpful had it been referring to psychological ones.

I took time to recover, I can't say exactly how long. I was hospitalised eight times in total. The good news, however, is that the last occasion was in 2000, and I've no intention of going back.

Turning around the kind of mess I was in is not an exact science. I would chance across a helpful book here, or take on board a bright adjustment to my prescription there, or find the will and the means to buy a home to call my own over here; all these things were steps along the way. And meeting Mrs G, someone to love and be loved by, was, of course, the best and biggest step of all. Being mad can become addictive, and the best way to break that habit is to want to be close to someone who can't abide it.

252

There were repercussions from my breakdown. The person I am today is the product of those aftershocks. There are ripples that I'm still only dimly aware of in the distance. That meant my career at Paston was troubled at times. But I would say I did the right thing in staying with teaching, and I hope my students would say the same.

I now count myself as disabled; I've had to accept that my psyche might spring unwelcome surprises on me until the day I die. I had to put circuit-breaker mechanisms in place at college (for example, choosing to work part-time). If my stress levels rose so that my mental health was threatened, I took a day off. It was far better from my students' point of view for me to be absent for a single day rather than be forced into missing work for six months. It was only seldom I needed to play this card.

I learned to protect my sleep patterns. I worked out the average number of hours that I felt a teacher should morally work each week, and stuck to that (unless I WANTED to do more).

Spending time with young people was a privilege, and I miss their company greatly. Sixteen to eighteen-year-olds, you have so much thrown at you these days. I'm not sure what I taught you, but I'm mightily thankful for what you taught me.

Tears

I don't cry a lot, which is why I remember my tears, and I recall them as holy ground. How many novels have made me cry? I can name them, and they occupy a sacred place on my bookshelf. True, I can count more films that have pushed me over the edge into tearfulness, but I'm more circumspect here; perhaps emotional strings are more easily pulled via the big screen. Then there's mathematics; I wonder, has this ever made me cry?

Might there be a certain self-importance in reflecting on one's own mathematical autobiography? An exercise in self–congratulation would indeed be worthless. But I'm the only person whose shoes I've ever fully occupied. When it comes to finding a subject for research, we are perfect: as willing to take part as we ourselves are, conveniently available (our diaries are always miraculously free at the same times as our own), and with a complete history to call on, we are our own best resource. And that includes the tears.

My first mathematical tears; I was six, living out a semi–colonial youth in Malaysia, an ex–pat in a freshly–independent nation that still needed my father's skills as a water engineer. I went to a school containing a rainbow of cultures. I recall being unable to make the leap from adding two–digit numbers to adding three–digit numbers, and the pain was acute. A laughing teacher pointed this sobbing pupil in the right direction, and I saw that the extra difficulties were not that great.

From six, a leap to twenty–six, and a time in my life without mathematics, as I left university to earn a living from music. I did not touch a maths book for four years. One day I pulled down a geometry text from a friend's bookshelf, and its pages made me weep. I'd neglected an important part of myself for too long.

Tears are not always regretful or painful. Aged forty–two, I was writing a GCSE worksheet on equations, when the mathematics suddenly took off. I had the sense of walking into a room that no–one had walked into before. Afterwards, awestruck, I scratched out a rough poem:

> *Three numbers, never bedfellows before,*
> *Are newly–wed into immortality.*
> *Linked secretly before the dawn of thought,*
> *This bizarre trinity is now revealed,*
> *With a few strokes of logic's pen.*
> *God's work or man's? Surely both,*
> *As a rabbit–hole yields beneath my foot,*
> *Soundlessly, tracelessly, opening new worlds of simplicity.*

Mathematics made me cry once more that day. I hope it will again soon.

Beckett Sums it Up

I'm standing in my Paston classroom for the last time. I've taken down and packed my mathematical mobile of red and black bars, I've plucked the maths books that are mine from the bookcase, and I've winnowed any potentially useful worksheets from files (I might HAVE to go back to work one day). Three thousand lessons have played themselves out within these four walls under my leadership. All that living bound up in this room; mysterious emotions run around my mind.

'One more thing...'

Stan Warinka, the Swiss tennis player, has these words from Samuel Beckett tattooed on his forearm:

Ever tried. Ever failed. No matter. Try Again. Fail again. Fail better.

It's certainly done him no harm, a three-time slam winner. The day I discovered what he'd done, I typed the words up onto a page and blu-tacked them to my classroom wall. As I stand now, I remember words about failure from a monk I once knew:

Our failures rot down to form the compost in which our successes grow.

I reach up and take the sheet of A4 down, wiping away the blu-tack from the surface to leave virgin wall. Ofsted would never understand. Maybe no one would.

With thanks to...

With thanks to Helen Williams, for commissioning me to write a column called *Correlation Street* that featured some of these articles. These appeared in *Mathematics Teaching*, the journal of the Association of Teachers of Mathematics.

With thanks to Colin Foster, who was also a big part of kicking these articles into shape for MT.

With thanks to Jo Knowsley, who oversaw my first batch of articles for the *Times Educational Supplement* (my thanks also goes to Michael Shaw and Ed Dorrell at the TES). The following pieces in this book appeared in the TES (possibly edited and under a different title) on these dates;

You must remember this; 21/10/11
Sex and Maths; 28/10/11
Mathematical hypnotherapy; 9/12/11
Brighter than me; 13/1/12
Who taught me that? 27/1/12
Michael; 24/2/12
Fermat's Last Theorem; 23/3/12
Look the part; 6/4/12
Gardening; 20/4/12
Grandparents; 27/4/12
Amy's mistake; 11/5/12
Avalanche; 1/6/12
Tom; 8/6/12
You surprise me; 27/7/12
Howlers; 26/10/12

Can girls do maths; 9/11/12
Little Bo Peep; 7/12/12
Then and now; 1/2/13
Mathematics is beautiful; 6/6/14
Writing upside down; 8/9/14
You can't make me; 30/1/15

With thanks to those who read drafts of this book, and fed back kindly.

With thanks to Mrs G, my denominatrix, for support way beyond the cause of duty in the production of this book, and for agreeing to appear in it.

And most importantly, with thanks to my students and colleagues at all the places I've taught:

Great Walstead Prep School in Lindfield,
Parkside Community College in Cambridge,
St Philip Howard School in Tower Hamlets,
St Dominic's Sixth Form College in Harrow,
Paston College in Norfolk,
and all my online and face-to-face tutees.

Disclaimer (this is possibly stronger than is necessary!)

This book is semi–autobiographical. The names of all living persons who've part–inspired characters in this book, however, will not be found here. Every character in this book is to some extent a composite character, based upon several people.

Some of the facts quoted in this book are in the public domain. There are also 'facts' described here that are exaggerations of known facts, and so are not strictly speaking true, although there may well be an element of truth in each case.

Nothing in this book should be taken as being an allegation against a real and living person or against a real institution unless it's true. All untrue 'facts' herein that could be construed as allegations should be regarded as part of the fictional side of this book.

Jonny Griffiths studied mathematics and education at Cambridge University, the Open University, and at the University of East Anglia. He taught maths at Paston Sixth Form College in Norfolk for over 20 years, being a Gatsby Teacher Fellow for the year 2005-6, when he created the popular *Risps* maths website.

Claims to fame include singing with the 1980s band *Harvey and the Wallbangers,* and playing the character of Stringfellow on *Playdays*, the television programme for children. He's had a theological book called *The 100-Word Bible* published by Darton, Longman and Todd.

An ebook of stories from his classroom was published by the Association of Teachers of Mathematics under the title *Correlation Street*, and he has also written many articles for the *Times Educational Supplement*. Pieces from these two sources can be found here in a revised form. The ATM has also published his work on proof, *The Proving Ground.*

He has worked recently for *Underground Mathematics*, Hodder, MEI and Integral. He was the originator and author of the A Level Maths competition Ritangle in 2016, which is now into its third year.